START ME UP

How That Band Got That Name They Got

MORGAN LOCKLEAR

Start Me Up
How That Band Got That Name They Got
by
Morgan Locklear

Copyright © 2022 Morgan Locklear
All rights reserved. No part of this publication may be reproduced, stored in a retrieval system, or transmitted in any form or by any means, electronic, mechanical, photocopying, recording, scanning, or otherwise, without the prior written permission of the author.
The author makes no representation, express or implied, with regard to the accuracy of the information contained in this publication and cannot accept any responsibility in law for any errors or omissions.

Published by Locklear Books
http://www.locklearbooks.com
info@locklearbooks.com.

Cover and Interior Design by Lindsey Gray
Cover and Interior Images from Adobe Stock Photos

First Edition 2022
ISBN: 979-8-9859871-2-6

Dedication

This book is dedicated to my friend, Sawyer White, and his whole awesome family - Jason, Jessala, Eli, and Jude.

TABLE OF CONTENTS

COPYRIGHT	
DEDICATION	
FOREWORD	1
INTRODUCTION	3
#	7
A	10
B	21
C	43
D	56
E	68
F	74
G	84
FRINGE SUB-SECTION	94
H	101
I	108
J	116
K	124
L	131
M	138
N	149
O	156
P	164
Q	173
R	175
S	186
T	199

U	208
V	212
W	216
X	224
Y	226
Z	230
ALSO FROM LOCKLEAR BOOKS	232
ABOUT THE AUTHOR	233

Foreword by Pat Todd

Thoughts to the Future, Roads to the Past

The music gave them their power, but in most cases, their names told you something about them and reflected who they were, where they came from, where they'd been, and who they wanted to become (Hell, even their showbiz was open-hearted!)

Muddy Waters, Howlin' Wolf, Blind Willie McTell, Bob Dylan, The Rolling Stones, Hank Williams & His Drifting Cowboys, The New York Dolls, The Ronettes, The Velvet Underground, Memphis Minnie, Merle Haggard & The Strangers, Roxy Music, The Replacements, Little Richard & The Upsetters, The Stooges, Bob Willis & His Texas Playboys, The Impressions, The Ramones, The Pretty Things, The Ike & Tina Turner Review, The Motor City Five, James Brown & The Famous Flames…I could go on and on…

Their names conjure up lives spent in music. Traditions, influences, the times they came up in, class, the stories they tell, and the stories told about them, the contradictions within them, and how we relate to them; something of the truth, I guess. (If there is such a thing.)

Think of all they spawned and the distance they and their music traveled. The stories and the images had a power that took me places. Right into the heart of mystery. Just hearing their music made life bigger, better, and sometimes even sadder. I will never forget this, and I carry it with me everywhere. It's in every conversation I have.

By now you're saying, "What's this guy talking about? Where's this going? What's the point?" Well, it all comes down to how and why you pick a name for a band. I think a name, and your music, for that matter, should be timeless. It should say something about who and what you are, or maybe who you think you are. Your name should be a window into what you believe and what's in your heart. It should show your relationship with the world. Of course, all of this should be in between the lines. After all, you don't want to give too much away. You've gotta keep something for the music…

Introduction by the Author

There has always been a built-in reverence for band names. From the revolutionary to the regrettable, a rock 'n' roll moniker can attain near mythical status. Even a made-up band name like, *Run For It Marty!* suddenly commands attention, if not intrigue. (Plus, I put it in italics, which looks nifty.)

Band names are slippery things. Many artists find it amusing to put out false origin stories, or worse, change their name to a symbol for fifteen years. (Just kidding, Prince.) When I found competing explanations for band names, I included them both. When I found boring or annoying explanations, I shared them with minimal guile. And if I found nothing but a single comment on Reddit, I slipped it in, and you'll never know the difference. (Just kidding, Voice Farm.)

In addition to band name origins, I've included hometowns, musical styles, some trivia, and a few related tangents. However, my favorite addition is the inclusion of *Signature Songs* and *Insight Songs*. The former are, of course, those songs most associated with the bands. *Insight songs* are my personal touch. These songs better reflect, or further reflect a band's overall style and sound. Singles don't always capture the true vibe of a band. Having said that, plenty of my *Insight Songs* are popular among fans. This is my attempt to showcase the heart of a band's musical soul. For your convenience, a playlist of Start Me Up: Insight Songs is available on Spotify.

Now, I couldn't include every post-punk-prog-rock band that ever existed. Germany alone would fill a hard drive, and flooding this book with obscure acts would no longer be fun to read. Think of it like flipping through a stranger's photo album; sure, it's somewhat fascinating for a while, but ultimately disconnecting, and therefore dissatisfying. But since this book recognizes those music fiends with an appetite for the underground, I've asked fellow musician, rock aficionado, and friend Chris Reid, to contribute a section of bands on the fringe. You can find him between Guns-n-Roses and Hard-Fi. The first of three sub-sections. The other two are surprises.

Have fun, friends. (And have fun friends.)

Stay tuned for other books in this series:

LOVE ME TWO TIMES: Debunking the Curse of the Sophomore Album, and Stuff About Bands With Only Two People In Them.

WE BUILT THIS CITY: A Tour Through The Greatest Regions of Rock.

And just in case I have to write a sequel to this book,
I HATE MYSELF FOR LOVIN' YOU: How Even More Bands Got The Names They Got.

Sources:

Any official band website available
YouTube interview videos
allmusic.com
amiright.com
billboard.com
classicbands.com
digitaldreamdoor.com
nme.com
bandnamesexplained.com
oldielyrics.com
rateyourmusic.com
The Why Not 100 Blog

# #

2NU

Our first group is from Seattle, Washington, and make for a great beginning story. 2nu, now resurrected as 2n2, began to get radio play in 1991 with their spoken word single, "This Is Ponderous" before the band was even officially a band. One local DJ introduced the song, but told his listeners that there was no band name because they were "too new." The band adapted the name and spelled it using the Prince approach.

All their songs are either instrumental or spoken word with music and sound effects. On paper it might seem gimmicky but their catalog, though small, is quite brilliant. Most songs are hilarious with a few haunting and emotional monoliths that act as anchors for their albums.

Signature songs: *This Is Ponderous, Spaz Attack*
Insight songs: *Two Outta Three, She, Frank's Chair, DDS Blues*

10CC

This legendary London, England, band formed in 1972 and was named by their producer, Jonathan King. He had a dream that he was standing in front of the Hammersmith Odeon, which is a huge venue. On the marquee were the words, "10cc The Best Band In The World."

Their music is classified as art rock, which is to say they're progressive and weird. Still, plenty of their songs are blues driven.
Signature songs: *Rubber Bullets, I'm Not In Love, Dreadlock Holiday*
Insight song: *Wall Street Shuffle*

100 MONKEYS

This quirky quintet is known to trade instruments both in the studio and on stage. It's quite the ballet to watch them step over cords and monitors to pass off guitars, drumsticks, microphone duties, and the like. Taking turns at the keyboard seems to be everyone's favorite spot in the rotation.

They're pretty experimental, even for a Los Angeles band, and they certainly have a goofy side, but they never stray too far from funk.

100 Monkeys took their name from the "Hundredth Monkey Phenomenon" described by Dr. Lyall Watson as a spontaneous and mysterious leap of consciousness that is achieved when a "critical mass" is reached. His 1979 book, *Lifetide,* describes a study done decades before where primatologists observed one monkey in the Japanese Macaques washing a potato. Soon, every monkey was allegedly washing potatoes. Soon after that, it was reported that the action was being repeated on separate islands by monkeys that had no apparent contact with each other. (This claim has since been widely

discredited by the way.)
Notable band member Jackson Rathbone played Jasper in the *Twilight* movies and quit the band in 2012. On his way out, his lawyers informed the remaining bandmates that they could no longer use the name.
Signature songs: *Sleeping Giants, Gus*
Insight songs: *Arizona, Wings On Fire*

311
This funk/reggae band named themselves after the police code for indecent exposure in their hometown of Omaha, Nebraska. They discovered this fact when their original guitarist was arrested for skinny dipping.
Signature songs: *Beautiful Disaster, Amber, Down*
Insight song: *Flowing*

THE 1975
Originally formed in Wilmslow, England, but now based in Manchester, this Brit pop/rock band has one of the most mysterious name selection stories. Lead singer Matt Healy once picked up a beatnik book at a yard sale and discovered several scribbles and words in the back. "…It was almost suicidal, and it was dated at the bottom 'June 1st, the 1975.' The use of the word 'the' really stuck with me. It was the perfect band name."
Signature songs: *Robbers, Girls, Somebody Else*
Insight song: *TOOTIMETOOTIMETOOTIME*

10,000 MANIACS

In 1981, this Jamestown, New York, band was called Still Life, and would even call themselves Burn Victims, before settling on a name inspired by the low-budget 1963 horror movie, *Two Thousand Maniacs*. They have a vocal/rock vibe led by noted singer Natalie Merchant.

Signature songs: *Because The Night, Like The Weather*
Insight songs: *Pit Viper, Peace Train*

A

A PERFECT CIRCLE
A Los Angeles band formed by guitarist Billy Howerdel and TOOL front man Maynard James Keenan. Their sound is certainly lighter than TOOL, but there's always room for intensity when Maynard is singing. Still, A Perfect Circle can be brutally vulnerable at times.
They took their name from the lyrics of their song, "Orestes," from the debut album, *Mer de Noms*. Maynard sings, "A Metaphor for a missing moment. Pull me into your perfect circle. One womb. One Shape. One Resolve. Liberate this will to release us all."
Signature songs: *The Hollow, Weak and Powerless*
Insight songs: *Gravity, 3 Libras*

A WILHELM SCREAM
New Bedford, Connecticut, is home to this hardcore band. Some of you may even be familiar with the name, although not through their music.
The Wilhelm Scream is a vocal effect famously used in hundreds of movies. It was recorded by Sheb Wooley for the Warner Bros. 1951 film *Distant Drums* but not used. It was officially dubbed the Wilhelm Scream two years later when it was included in the movie *Charge at Feather River*. The scream is heard when the character Private

Wilhelm gets shot in the thigh by an arrow.

For a crystal-clear example, watch the scene in *Toy Story* when Woody knocks Buzz out the window with the desk lamp. Buzz's scream is the Wilhelm Scream. You will no doubt realize that you have heard it many times before.

Signature song: *Born A Wise Man*

Insight songs: *Famous Friends And Fashion Drunks, The Horse*

ABBA

Sweden's most famous band—all apologies to Ace of Base—and they start us off with the formula of combining the band members' names. In this case, ABBA is an acronym for their first names; Agnetha (Faltskog), Bjorn (Ulvaeus), Benny (Anderson), and Anni-Frid (Lyngstad). ABBA remain disco legends fifty years after the fact.

Signature song: *Dancing Queen*

Insight song: *Gimme! Gimme! Gimme! (A Man After Midnight)*

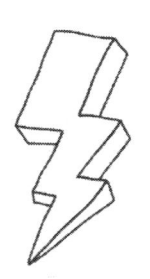

AC/DC

Band founders and Sydney siblings Angus and Malcolm Young originally came from Scotland, and started their band after their older brother encouraged them. Their sister, Margret, suggested using a term marked on her sewing machine after she heard them play, AC/DC. The term is used to denote that the device uses Alternating

Current and Direct Current electricity to operate. The name perfectly fit their energetic hard rock sound.
Signature songs: *You Shook Me All Night Long, Dirty Deeds, Back In Black*
Insight song: *Big Balls*

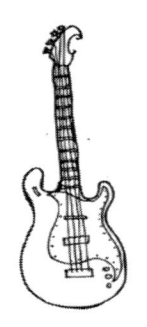

ACE OF BASE

Wow! Only a few bands in, and two of them are from Sweden! Spoiler alert: Sweden does not finish as strongly as it starts. But only a Swedish band would name themselves for being the masters of their basement. These three siblings, along with singer and keyboardist Ulf Ekberg, recorded their debut pop music album beneath a pet shop and their name became Ace of Base.
Signature songs: *The Sign, All That She Wants*
Insight song: *Beautiful Life*

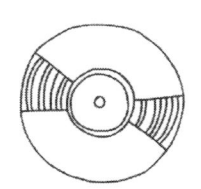

AEROSMITH

Drummer Joey Kramer liked the blending of two old-fashioned terms, aero and smith, and wrote the name on his high school books. Later, when he pitched it as the name for a newly forming rock band, the rest of the group thought he was referring to the Sinclair Lewis book, *Arrowsmith*. He was not. These Boston boys are one of the few seventies bands that survived into the eighties, nineties, and beyond.
Signature songs: *Walk This Way, Sweet Emotion*
Insight song: *Big Ten Inch Record*

A-HA

Lead singer Morten Harket saw this name in bandmate Pal Waaktaar's notebook as a song title and liked it. Norway's biggest band—all apologies to The September When—discovered that a-ha means the same thing in nearly every language. (A pleasant discovery or surprise.) Their other choice would have been Taxi, which also means the same thing in nearly every language, and not a bad second choice for a band name.

A-ha's vocal pop sound, coupled with a brilliant debut video for "Take On Me," propelled them into super stardom. A lot of people don't know that they've recorded over ten studio albums since then. All of which are excellent, by the way.

Signature songs: *Take On Me, The Living Daylights*
Insight songs: *East of the Sun West Of The Moon, Cozy Prisons, Lamb To The Slaughter, Analogue, Dragonfly*

AIR SUPPLY

Five years before signing with a label, Graham Russel saw the name on a billboard in a dream. He was an Englishman but formed the band with Australian lead singer, Russel Hitchcock. Their vocal style and piercing lyrics are wholly underrated.

Signature songs: *All Out Of Love, Making Love Out Of Nothing At All*
Insight song: *Sweet Dreams*

ALABAMA

This one might seem obvious, like the kind of paragraph you might skip in a collection like this, especially if you weren't into country music. But this happens to be one of the sweetest and most organic stories in the collection. For starters, it mostly takes place in South Carolina, but does indeed begin in Alabama with a trio of cousins who all grew up around Fort Payne.

Randy Owen, lead vocals and rhythm guitar, and Teddy Gentry, bassist and vocalist, lived on separate cotton farms around Lookout Mountain but sang in church together and learned to play guitar together. Once they teamed up with another regular at family gatherings, Jeff Cook, (lead guitar, keyboards, fiddle, vocals) they knew, along with everyone else, that they had something special.

Alabama is still the most successful country band in history, and it all started with the cousins winning a high school talent show by playing a Merle Haggard song. They performed under the name Young Country but, after they moved to South Carolina to pursue music full time, later changed their name to Wildcountry.

Here's where the sweet part comes in. When they played gigs, Teddy Gentry would hang up a sign on stage with the name of their home state on it. This caused most people to refer to them as the Alabama band, but they didn't officially change their name until 1977 when they signed a contract with GRT records.

Signature songs: *Tennessee River, Song Of The South, Dixieland Delight*
Insight song: *Pass It On Down*

ALICE COOPER
Okay, here's the visual. A sweet little girl holding a hatchet behind her back. The band came up with the name and an elaborate story about a Ouija board and the past life of lead singer Vince Furnier. As expected, everyone just assumed that Alice Cooper was the name of the front man. Vince eventually took the name and went solo.
The band started out in Phoenix, Arizona, in 1964 and rocked hard for eleven years.
Signature song: *School's Out For Summer*
Insight song: *Billion Dollar Babies*

ALIEN ANT FARM
This band name came to bassist Terry Corso in a daydream about how Earth could be the experiment of beings from another planet. He's from Riverside, California, if that helps explain anything. The band has a punk/pop thing going on, and their biggest single was a cover of Michael Jackson's "Smooth Criminal."
Signature song: *Smooth Criminal (cover)*
Insight song: *Yellow Pages*

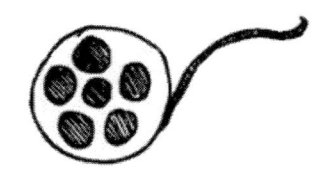

ALPHAVILLE

These bandmates coalesced in Berlin, Germany, in 1982 but their lead singer had already written their biggest hit three years before. Marion Gold came up with "Big In Japan" when he first heard Holly Johnson's band of the same name. This was, of course, before Johnson went on to front Frankie Goes To Hollywood.

Alphaville's other big hit "Forever Young" was the original name of the band before they chose to pay homage to something else they loved. This time it would be the 1965 science fiction French film by Jean-Luc Godard. London based *Time Out* magazine called the movie, *Alphaville*, "a dazzling amalgam of film noir and science fiction." The band's music fits their name, not that they have a bunch of sci-fi noises or anything, and not that there's anything wrong with that, but their sound feels old and new at the same time.

Signature songs: *Big In Japan, Forever Young, Sounds Like A Melody*

Insight song: *Summer In Berlin*

ANIMAL COLLECTIVE

Rolling Stone once declared that Animal Collective challenges their listeners. The statement was made within a review for their soul boggling 2012 album, *Centipede Hz*. An album which had me imagining that it was created by aliens who had heard music from Earth and, assuming that it was an element of our language, responded in kind.

The Baltimore, Maryland, collective is just that, an interchangeable yet consistently experimental group of artists, DJs, producers, and musicians. One of the more famous collaborators is Panda Bear. Maybe that's why they went with Animal Collective. I could not find an official story, which means I ordinarily would have just left them out of the book. But they're a personal favorite, and I was light on bands with names that began with the letter *A*.

Signature song: Summertime Clothes
Insight songs: Monkey Riches, Pulleys, Applesauce, Golden Gal, Prester John, Who Could Win A Rabbit

ANTHRAX

Most of the heavy metal bands of the eighties came from the West Coast, but these New York boys opened up a biology book, picked a "sufficiently evil sounding" name, and rocked their way into the history books.

Signature song: Madhouse
Insight song: Monster At The End

THE ANTI-DENTITES

From Hamden, Connecticut. Woo! Hoo! Representing for the 203 (and the 475). This punk band took their name from the TV show *Seinfeld*.

Kramer accuses Jerry of being an anti-dentite after he complains that his dentist, played by Bryan Cranston, switched to Judaism in order to expand upon the kind of jokes he could tell at the office. "You're a RAVING anti-dentite!" Kramer famously yells.
Signature song: *Tortoise And The Hare*
Insight song: *Sing It If You Know It*

ART OF NOISE

Music producer Trevor Horn was one of the first engineers to purchase a new piece of 1979 technology from Australia, the Fairlight CMI Sampler. It was very much like a drum machine with pitch control. Horn formed a production team that racked up such credits as ABC's debut album, *The Lexicon of Love*, and *Welcome To The Pleasuredome* by Frankie Goes To Hollywood.

In '82 Trevor Horn's solo work drew such attention from his record company that, one by one, members of the recently disbanded Yes were brought in to play. Eventually, Horn was asked to join the group and make his progressive songs the bedrock of their comeback album. (It's not like they didn't trade out band members like VHS tapes anyway.) The album *90125*, named so for its catalog number at Atco Records, became the band's most commercially successful release to date.

Meanwhile, Trevor and his production group decided to

create their own sample based musical group. They took their name from the 1913 manifesto, *The Art of Noises* by Italian futurist Luigi Russolo. Their debut release, *Into Battle*, has some of the same sample sounds as the aforementioned Yes album.
Signature songs: *Peter Gunn (Cover), Moments In Love*
Insight songs: *The Army Now, Snapshot*

ARTFUL DODGER
Armed with a name taken straight from the pages of the Charles Dickens classic, *Oliver Twist*, this band put their own twist on music beginning in 1973. From their home in Fairfax, Virginia, they produced highly harmonized songs that, although critically applauded, never quite hit with mainstream listeners.
Signature songs: *Scream, Wayside*
Insight song: *Honor Among Thieves*

AS I LAY DYING
San Diego, California, isn't the usual place to find a metalcore band, but there they are. They're close enough to Los Angeles to make sense though. Those Southern California bands are either trippy or intense. Sometimes both, but not these guys. As I Lay Dying is a line from the 1930 William Faulkner novel of the same name.
Signature song: *Nothing Left*
Insight song: *My Own Grave*

ATREYU

Wow! Two metalcore bands in a row, *and* they're both from unlikely locations. Yorba Linda is in Orange County, California, home to many great punk and metal bands. So, maybe it isn't as big a stretch as San Diego, but Yorba Linda sounds like a place that would only produce vegans who play acoustic guitar while barefoot on stage.

Atreyu is the name of a young warrior in the 1984 film, *The Neverending Story*.

Signature song: *Ain't Love Grand*
Insight song: *Ex's & Oh's*

AWOLNATION

In high school, bandleader and sole member Aaron Bruno used to leave social gatherings without saying goodbye. He would just sort of fade away into the L.A. fray. This earned him a nickname borrowed from the military, AWOL. (Absent Without Official Leave.) You can see how he came up with the name from there. The sound of AWOLNATION is hard to pin down. Heavy at times, but smooth as butter on other occasions. I'm a fan.

Signature songs: *Sail, Run, The Best*
Insight songs: *Jump On My Shoulders, Knights Of Shame, Handyman, Mayday!!! Fiesta Fever*

B

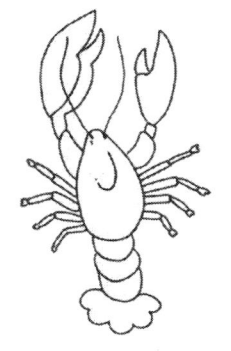

B-52s

As this band was forming in Athens, Georgia, in the seventies bandmates Kate Pierson and Cindy Wilson were often wearing beehive hairdos, also known as B-52s. The style's nickname became the band's name.

It might be easy to dismiss the B-52s as a novelty band due to their zany musical attack but they are, in fact, legends in the biz.

Signature songs: *Love Shack, Rock Lobster, Strobe Light*
Insight songs: *Planet Claire, Deadbeat Club, Junebug*

BACKSTREET BOYS

These hip-hop harmonizers hail from Orlando, Florida, and named themselves after a bygone flea market known as the Backstreet Market. They used to hang out there as kids.

Signature songs: *I Want It That Way, Everybody*
Insight song: *Larger Than Life*

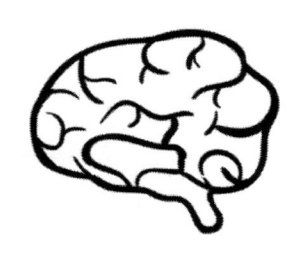

BAD BRAINS

Every city has its own sound and, sometimes, that sound is credited to a single band. For Washington, D.C., that sound is Bad Brains. These innovators are revered in the punk community even though their music is much more. They include elements of funk, jazz, and world music, and took their name from the 1978 Ramones song "Bad Brain."

Signature songs: **I Against I, Rise**
Insight song: **Sacred Love**

BAD COMPANY

With a name taken from the 1972 film, *Bad Company*, this rock band formed a year later in Surrey County, England. Bad Company is known as a supergroup, which is a band made up of members from other successful bands. In the case of Bad Company, their members came from the bands Free, Mott The Hoople, and King Crimson.

They were managed by the same guy who managed Led Zeppelin, and their debut album was the first release on Led Zeppelin's newly created label, Swan Song Records.

Signature songs: *Feel Like Makin' Love, Rock 'n' Roll Fantasy*
Insight song: *Bad Company*

BAD ENGLISH

Another supergroup! This one was made up of members of Journey and The Babys. They were already recording an album before they even had a name. Bandmates played billiards during break times in the studio and, since at least some of them were lousy players, the term "Bad English" was often used. English is the word used to describe the spin of the ball. Bad English usually results in a terrible shot.
Signature song: *When I See You Smile*
Insight song: *Best of What I Got*

BAD RELIGION

None of these band members had graduated from high school when they recorded their first album. It sold 10,000 copies in about two years. Of course, the name Bad Religion had shock value, always a commodity on the punk scene, but they knew a name like that would also define them. They would be standing for the abject rejection of blind conformity to all poisoned doctrines, governments, and systems of control. Their music was more intelligent than that of their contemporaries, then and now.

Bad Religion guitarist Brett Gurewitz started Epitaph Records, which is now a big player in alternative music. (Although they never got back to me about the name

origins of Teenage Wrist).
Signature songs: *No Control, 21st Century Digital Boy, Sorrow, American Jesus*
Insight songs*: Struck A Nerve, Automatic Man*

BAKER GURVITZ ARMY

Once again, we're treated to a band that combined its members' names. Ginger Baker, who is a celebrated drummer, and brothers Adrian and Paul Gurvitz added a militant touch to their name—a holdover from their previous band, Three Man Army. The band was formed in England after Cream split up, and Blind Faith fizzled. That's right, another supergroup!
Signature song: *Mad Jack*
Insight song: *People*

BANANARAMA

This plucky female vocal trio was known for singing largely in unison. Harmony singing, like that of the Andrew Sisters, has a very different vibe than everyone reinforcing the same note. It makes for a more modern sound, and Bananarama were a new wave band for sure. These musicians grew up in London and took part of their name from the Roxy Music song "Pyjamarama." The other part came from the English children's television show *The Banana Splits*. Speaking of splits, when Siobhan Fahey left the group in

1988, she formed a new band called Shakespears Sister.
Signature songs: *Cruel Summer, I Heard A Rumor, Venus*
Insight songs: *Love in the First Degree, Nathan Jones*

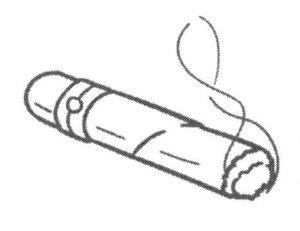

THE BANANA CONVENTION
This is the fictional band Greg Brady joins in a late episode of *The Brady Bunch*. It's the episode where he gets caught smoking. I include it here to illustrate how dirty that name really is. I believe a banana convention was the 1970s equivalent of what we would call a sausage party today. The sentiment is nothing new, of course. Ancient Romans drew dicks on everything.
Signature (and only) song: *Till I Met You* (Actually written by Barry Williams)

BARENAKED LADIES
Once, when future band members Ed Robertson and Steven Page were at a Bob Dylan concert they discussed band names, and this one came up. While it would certainly get them noticed, it was also false advertising.
Later, Ed's band broke up just before they were to play in a Scarborough, Canada, area battle of the bands. When the event coordinator called to confirm his slot, Ed told him that the band had changed their name to Barenaked Ladies. Ed then called Steven and asked him to play the show with him under the name they had discussed. Steven said yes, and the band was born.

In true Canadian band fashion, they are great singers, write romantic and funny songs alike, and play great live shows.
Signature songs: *If I Had a Million Dollars, One Week*
Insight songs: *Hello City, Wrap Your Arms Around Me, The Old Apartment, What A Good Boy, Box Set, Straw Hat And Old Dirty Hank*

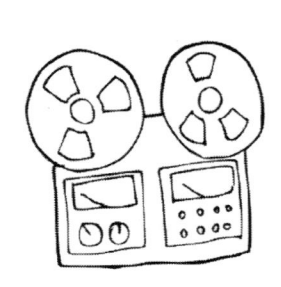

BAUHAUS
These Berlin post-punk rockers named themselves after the German Bauhaus art movement. In fact, they were originally called Bauhaus 1919, but shortened their name in 1979 just before they released their magnum-opus, "Bela Lugosi's Dead."
Signature song: *Bela Lugosi's Dead*
Insight song: *Ziggy Stardust*

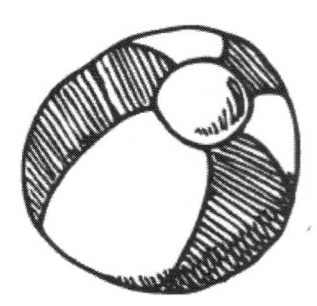

THE BEACH BOYS
When these California harmonizers recorded their first record for Candix Records, they performed under the name The Pendletones. Since their song was called "Surfin'" a promotions worker, named Russ Regan, changed the band's name to something he felt was more surf-culture related.

The band was furious with the change but, due to a limited budget, the records were released as they were printed. The song was a hit, and the name stuck.

Signature songs: *Barbara Ann, I Get Around, Good Vibrations, Help Me Rhonda, Surfin' USA*
Insight songs: *Darlin'*

BEASTIE BOYS

The pride of New York City, and with good reason. This band fused punk, hip-hop, and jazz to become one of the most influential acts of their era and beyond.

In 1979, they were called The Young Aborigines and had a successful local EP, *Polly-Wog Stew*.

A line-up change in the early eighties also came with a name change. Beastie Boys was chosen mostly because it sounded primal and dangerous. It was meant to be a temporary name for a temporary three-man line-up.

According to a Mike D interview, Beastie is an acronym that stands for "Boys Entering Anarchistic States Towards Inner Excellence". This may be a joke or, at least, something derived later in their career.

Signature songs: *(You Gotta) Fight For Your Right, Sabotage, Intergalactic, Hey Ladies*
Insight songs: *She's Crafty, An Open Letter To NYC, Pow, Pass The Mic*

THE BEATLES

I believe that when someone asks "What is your favorite band?" there is no wrong answer. Music is subjective, after all. We like what we like. However, when someone asks "What is the best band?" there is only one answer, The Beatles. Their contribution to the progression of modern music cannot be understated. People who disagree haven't bothered to understand what was happening at the time or how, even today, musicians are influenced by The Beatles in everything from sound engineering to songwriting. No, I am not a superfan. I didn't even start taking The Beatles seriously until I was in my thirties. But when I understood, I understood.

Their name began as an homage to Buddy Holly and The Crickets, that's why they chose to name their band after an insect. Beetles struck a chord with them, but John Lennon changed the spelling to reference the "beat" in a song. Yep. The best band in history has the worst pun in history for a name.

Although they were from Liverpool, England, they cut their teeth performing in Hamburg, Germany, which is still a common practice today.

Signature songs: *Hey Jude, I Want to Hold Your Hand, Twist and Shout, Back In The U.S.S.R., Revolution, Yellow Submarine, Octopus's Garden*
Insight songs: *Elinore Rigby, Fixing A Hole*

BEE GEES

Popular opinion is that Bee Gees stands for Brothers Gibb, but there were many other B.G.'s in their lives that these initials actually refer to. One such person is Bill Goode, a friend who helped them out in their early career when they were a five-piece rock band called The Rattlesnakes. Other B.G.'s are Bill Gates (not that one), their producer, and Barbara Gibb, their mother and original producer.

They were all born on the Isle of Man and partly raised in Manchester, England, before moving on to Brisbane, Australia, where they began their disco days as a band.

Signature song: *Stayin' Alive*
Insight song: *If I Can't Have You*

BETTY'S NOT A VITAMIN

These are Florida boys from Clearwater Beach, which is right on the Gulf of Mexico. West of Tampa, Clearwater Beach is basically *in* the Gulf. No kidding! There's a Walgreens, an aquarium, and, of course, a Cooters Restaurant & Bar, all just chillin' in the Gulf of Mexico, and only a few miles away from at least sixteen roller coasters. It must be some kind of paradise, but this band's music is not as chill as the place they come from.

Now, as to their name, the Bayer company launched a vitamin craze in the seventies with Flintstones Vitamins.

But did you know there is no Betty character included? There's Fred, Wilma, Pebbles, Barney, Bam-Bam, Dino, even the Flintstones car, but no Betty Rubble. The reason given by Bayer was that the Betty vitamin had a very thin waist, and kept breaking during production, so they took her out.

Signature song: *Last Ride*
Insight song: *Jesus, Nixon And Elvis*

BIG AUDIO DYNAMITE

Mick Jones left The Clash because he was more and more drawn to electronic influences in his music. The rest of the band let him get it out of his system with the positively gigantic three-record album *Sandinista* but Mick kept going in a different direction. They recorded another solid record together, *Combat Rock*, which gave them their biggest hit, but Mick left soon after.

Jones spent the next year or so running with the London band General Public and forming his first post-Clash group, Top Risk Action Company, which he promptly folded. But that name gives us insight into his thinking. He wanted a zazzy name to go with his zazzy new sound. Mick then formed a band with film director Don Letts, and the name they chose was intended to describe the sound of their music as literally as possible.

Signature song: *Rush*
Insight song: *The Bottom Line*

BIG BAD VOODOO DADDY

Started in Ventura, California, by Scotty Morris. He named his swing band from something written to him by blues guitar legend, Albert Collins. Albert signed a poster, "To Scotty, the big bad voodoo daddy." According to Morris, when it came time to name his swing band, he only had one choice. After all, the name was handed to him by royalty.
Signature song: You & Me & The Bottle Makes 3
Insight song: Maddest Kind Of Love

BIG BROTHER AND THE HOLDING COMPANY

The psychedelic music scene began in the mid-sixties in San Francisco, California. It produced such great bands as Grateful Dead and Jefferson Airplane. Big Brother And The Holding Company had a secret weapon in the form of their amazing lead singer, Janis Joplin. Their sophomore album, *Cheap Thrills*, is considered one of the best ever recorded. They took their name from George Orwell's novel, *1984*.
Signature songs: Ball And Chain, Heartache People
Insight song: Down On Me

BIKINI KILL

A lot of interesting bands have come from Washington state. These rebel girls are from the capital city of Olympia. Their music was sneered at in the 1990s, but like wine, cheese, and episodes of *The X-Files*, they only improve with age.

The band name was first used as the title of a Zine, (underground magazine), started by members of the band in 1990. Kathleen Hanna and company are actually credited with coining the term "Girl Power", which is defined as the idea that women and girls should be confident, make decisions, and achieve things independently of men. Bikini Kill is another expression of conveying girl power. The band's shows were safe places for women, and the group often addressed violence against women in their punk music and at their performances.

Signature song: *Rebel Girl*
Insight song: *White Boy*

BILLY TALENT

The 27th best-selling Canadian rock band of all time, Billy Talent is from Mississauga, Canada. They have a punk/power pop sound with the usual Canadian sense of humor. In fact, they were part of the underground Toronto music scene as *Pezz* before changing their name.

The name Billy Talent was taken from the 1993 Michael Turner book, *Hard Core Logo*. Billy is a character in the novel which is about being in a rock band. (Specifically, Michael Turner's short-lived band called Hard Core Miners.*)*

Signature songs: *Devil On My Shoulder, Surrender*
Insight song: *I Beg To Differ*

THE BLACK CROWES
The band was founded in Georgia in 1984 by brothers Chris Robinson and Rich Robinson. Six years later, their cover of Otis Redding's "Hard To Handle" made them a global success. In the beginning, they called themselves Mr. Crowe's Garden, after a fairy tale, but eventually changed that to The Black Crowes. As you can see, they kept the irregular spelling. Blues rock is their bread and butter.

Signature songs: *Hard To Handle, She Talks To Angels*
Insight song: *Jealous Again*

BLACK EYED PEAS
Once upon a time, members of this Los Angeles based group were in a band called A Tribe Beyond Nation and signed to Eazy-E's record label, Ruthless Records. After the legendary rapper's death, the group briefly became the Black Eyed Pods but later changed to Black Eyed Peas. As Will.i.am explained in an interview, (and also written on the cover of their fourth album, *Monkey Business*), the name was chosen because their music is "food for your soul."

Signature songs: *Let's Get It Started, Pump It, My Humps*
Insight songs: *MAMACITA, The Time (Dirty Bit)*

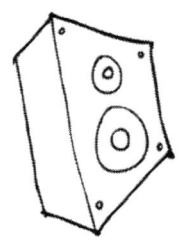

BLACK FLAG

If the white flag is the symbol of surrender, the black flag is the symbol of conquer. These L.A. rebels chose this savvy name and became legends on the punk scene almost immediately. Citing philosophical differences, lead singer Keith Morris quit to start his own band, Circle Jerks. Henry Rollins, a regular show goer and enthusiastic band friend, auditioned for the job. His onstage persona propelled them as punk legends.

Signature songs: Nervous Breakdown, Rise Above, My
Insight songs: Wasted, Jealous Again, Depression

THE BLACK KEYS

This Akron, Ohio, indie rock duo got their name from a family friend, Alfred McMore, who was diagnosed with schizophrenia and would leave incoherent messages on their phone's answering machine. He would often refer to people he didn't like as "black keys" or "D flats."

Signature songs: Tighten Up, Gold On The Ceiling
Insight song: Lonely Boy, For The Love Of Money

BLACK REBEL MOTORCYCLE CLUB

These sons of San Francisco play a bluesy kind of rock, and took their name from the 1953 film *The Wild Ones*.

Signature songs: *Beat The Devil's Tattoo, Ain't No Easy Way (Dirty Version)*
Insight song: *What Ever Happened To My Rock And Roll*

BLACK SABBATH

This Ozzy Osbourne fronted band is known as a pioneer of heavy metal music. But they started out innocently enough in Birmingham, England, as the Polka Tulk Blues Band. They also called themselves Earth for a time. While playing some shows in Germany in 1969, they saw that a theatre was showing the 1963 horror anthology film *Black Sabbath*. Seeing that name on the marquee was all they needed.

Signature songs: *War Pigs, Iron Man*
Insight songs: *The Wizard, Changes*

BLIND MELON

Although this alternative rock band formed in Los Angeles, California, most of the members are from Mississippi. They took their band name from the Cheech and Chong character, Blind Melon Chitlin', which was, in itself, a reference to 1920s blues legend Blind Lemon Jefferson.

Signature song: *No Rain*
Insight song: *Galaxie*

BLINK 182

These punk rockers are from Poway, California, which is between Los Angeles and San Diego, but a lot closer to San Diego. Band founder Tom DeLonge thought of the name Blink after they decided to ditch the name Duct Tape.

They performed under the name Blink for the first half of the nineties, but discovered that it was already being used by an Irish electronica artist. So, they added the 182 because that's the number of times Al Pacino says the word *fuck* in the movie *Scarface*.

Signature songs: *All The Small Things, I Miss You*
Insight song: *Los Angeles*

BLOOD MERIDIAN

Just in case you were wondering if we'd have any Canadian alternative country bands in this collection, here you go! Hailing from Vancouver, Canada, Blood Meridian's music is good, but just as bleak-hearted as their name suggests. *Blood Meridian* is the title of Cormac McCarthy's 1985 novel. It's a dingy tale of a crumpled world with absolutely zero kittens in it.

Signature song: *Kick Up The Dust*
Insight song: *Shit Word*

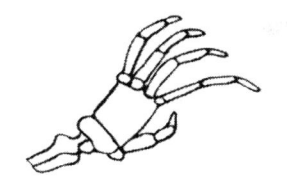

BLOODHOUND GANG

King Of Prussia sounds like a pretty good name for a band, but that's actually the Pennsylvania town these punk rockers hail from. Before settling into their niche, they once played hip-hop as Band Chamber 8.

The name was taken from a PBS show called *3-2-1 Contact*, and *The Bloodhound Gang* was a show within that show about a kid's detective agency. Sing it with me now, Gen X-ers! "Whenever there's trouble, we're there on the double, we're the Bloodhound Gang."

Signature song: *The Bad Touch*
Insight songs: *The Ballad Of Chasey Lain, Three Point One Four*

BLUE OYSTER CULT

Stony Brook, New York, 1967. A group of musicians were jamming in a communal house on Long Island and overheard by rock critic, Sandy Pearlman. He offered to manage the band and wanted them to be the American answer to Black Sabbath.

Their name came from Pearlman's poetry, which describes the Blue Oyster Cult as a group of aliens secretly guiding Earth's history. He came up with the name after seeing Blue Point oysters on a menu. His collection of works, *Imaginos*, was extensively used on their 1988 concept album of the same name.

Before they took that name, the band was called Soft

White Underbelly, taken from a statement Winston Churchill made about Italy in World War II. Other names they had before settling on Blue Oyster Cult were Stalk Forrest Group, Oaxaca, The Disciples, Santos Sisters, and Travesty.

Signature songs: *(Don't Fear) The Reaper, Burnin' For You*

Insight song: *Take Me Away*

BOMBAY BICYCLE CLUB

This is one of the coolest band names in this book, and if you haven't heard their music, do yourself the favor. They're funky and loose musically, but with emotionally charged themes. They have that Brit grit mixed with a little Yank stank. Like if Oasis and Weezer had a baby. However, it's the East End of the pond that gets to take credit for them. (That means they're from England.)

Three of four band members met and played together at high school and called themselves The Canals. They're from Crouch End in North London and named their band after an Indian restaurant chain.

Signature songs: *Always Like This, Luna*

Insight song: *Eat, Sleep, Wake (Nothing But You)*

BONZO DOG DOO DAH BAND

Also known as the Bonzo Dog Band, and even The Bonzos. Their name might be unfixed but their formation couldn't be more concrete. The band fused on the night of September 25th, 1962, just after watching the transatlantic broadcast of the boxing match between Floyd Patterson and Sonny Liston. They were watching at 164a Resendale Road, West Dulwich which, ironically, is in South London.

Their music is more jazzy than psychedelic, and very comical. If Monty Python was a band instead of a comedy troupe, they would sound like this. Bonzo Dog Doo Dah Band chose their name using a European avant-garde movement method wherein they cut up paper with word segments written on them and rearranged them to form new phrases. One of the words created was *Dada*, the very name of the avant-garde movement they were borrowing from. Dadaism has its roots in a Zurich nightclub called Cabaret Voltaire, circa 1916.

Furthermore, Bonzo The Dog was already a popular British cartoon character, so it delighted them when his name came up as well. Some people might have been scared away by choosing such a wacky name but these blokes were fearless.

Their song "Death Cab For Cutie" was featured on a season one episode of the British TV show "Do Not Adjust Your Set" which gave them a ton of attention, including from The Beatles. Later, an American band would name

themselves after that hit single.
Signature songs: *Death Cab For Cutie, I'm The Urban Spaceman*
Insight song: *My Pink Half Of The Drainpipe*

BOWLING FOR SOUP

A punk band from Wichita Falls, Texas? Sure, why not? You can almost hear the southern influence in their rock/punk sound. These funny fellows kept at it until they finally found fame with their sixth album, *The Great Burrito Extortion Case*. They also perform the *Jimmy Neutron* theme song.

They took their name from a Steve Martin comedy routine called "Bowling For Dollars".

Signature songs: *1985, High School Never Ends*
Insight songs: *Punk Rock 101, Here's Your Freakin' Song*

BR549

Previously spelled BR5-49, which goes right into the how and why they got their name in the first place. It came from the CBS television show, *Hee-Haw*. One running sketch starred Junior Samples as a used car salesman. His telephone number was listed as: BR-549.

In order to avoid a lawsuit, this Tennessee country trio, already established musicians from other bands, changed the location of the dash mark and eventually got rid of it altogether.

Signature song: *Cherokee Boogie*
Insight song: *Me-n-Opie*

BREAD

This band of soft rockers was mostly formed in Los Angeles and already signed with Elektra Records, but without a name. One day, stuck in traffic together behind a Wonder Bread truck, the name suddenly came to them. When their first album flopped they added a bassist, which usually solves the problem.

Signature songs: Baby I'm-A Want You, If
Insight song: Everything I Own

BUFFALO SPRINGFIELD

One of my favorite origin stories in this book. Formed by Neil Young, Stephen Stills, and Richie Furay, to name a few, this classic rock band took their name from a heavy asphalt roller they saw parked on the street in Los Angeles.

Signature song: For What It's Worth (Something Happening Here)
Insight song: Mr. Soul

BUSH

Named for their home district in West London, called Shepherd's Bush, the band found problems in Canada where another band by that name already existed. For a while, they were Bush X in the Great White North but were able to work out a deal with the copyright holder after making donations to Canadian charities. Their brand of alternative,

yet approachable music has been remarkably consistent, although they've never matched the kind of attention of their debut album, *Sixteen Stone*.
Signature songs: *Everything Zen, Come Down*
Insight songs: *Alien, Flowers On A Grave, Ghost In The Machine*

BUTTHOLE SURFERS

A few bands took their names from early songs they wrote. The song in question here is indeed called "Butthole Surfer". Legend has it that a venue announcer mistook the song for the band's name, and it stuck. These punk-comedy musicians are from San Antonio, Texas, and originally chose a different band name for each show. Two examples: Ashtray Baby Head and Nine Foot Worm Makes Home Food.
Signature songs: *Pepper, Dracula From Houston, The Annoying Song*
Insight song: *Cough Syrup*

C

CAGE THE ELEPHANT
These Kentucky rockers were playing a gig in Tennessee when a crazy person grabbed singer Matthew Shultz and gave him a hug. Among other things, this man reportedly told Matthew, "You have to cage the elephant! You have to cage the elephant!"
They have an alternative sound and they can be quite experimental. Lyrically dense yet not cumbersome. Their fifth album, *Social Cues*, won the Grammy for Best Rock Album 2020.
Signature song: Ain't No Rest for the Wicked
Insight songs: Broken Boy, It's Just Forever, Sweetie Little Jean, Night Running

CAKE
There are a few definitions of the word "cake" and only one applies to this band. It's not the yummy dessert, nor is it meant to describe when some task is super easy to do, as in "that was a cakewalk." Instead, the cake these Sacramento, California, boys refer to with their name is when something gets caked on your shoe.
Signature songs: I Will Survive (Cover), Short Skirt / Long Jacket
Insight songs: Stickshifts And Safetybelts, No Phone

CAMPER VAN BEETHOVEN

This band moniker is a pun. It combines famous German composer Ludwig van Beethoven and, you guessed it, a camper van. As it turns out, this was the perfect name for the innovative and short-lived group.

They're from Redlands, California, which makes this the part in the book where I realize a trend that bands from California really are more trippy.

In what surely must be a record for alphabetically adjacent band names created by the same musician, David Lowery fronts another band, Cracker, which is only a handful of spots further along, right after the poem I share in the Counting Crows entry.

Signature song: *Take The Skinheads Bowling*
Insight song: *Where The Hell Is Bill?*

CANDLEBOX

According to guitarist Peter Klett, singer Kevin Martin's girlfriend lit a candle inside the glove box of drummer Scott Mercado's uncle's van. Predictably, the candle melted the dash and Kevin yelled, "It's a glove box, not a candle box!" These Seattle grunge rockers knew a good band name when they heard one.

Signature songs: *You, Don't You*
Insight songs: *Arrow, Cover Me*

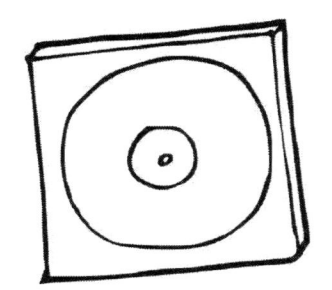

CARBON LEAF

This very cool name was the result of a brainstorming/hiking/rafting trip in Tennessee taken by guitarist Terry Clark and singer Berry Privett. The words *carbon* and *leaf* came up independently, but stuck to each other. When the name was printed on flyers for their first gig, a house party in their hometown of Richmond, Virginia, they knew they had a winner. The name is brainy, but edgy. Mysterious, but simple. It's a great band name for a very talented and much underexposed group.

Their musical style might be one of the hardest to put into words. Alternative, but not always. Acoustic, but not always. Bluesy, but not always, and with some of the best lyrics in the business. Second only to Iron & Wine, and Ani DiFranco.

Signature songs: *Life Less Ordinary, The Friendship Song (From the movie Curious George 2)*

Insight songs: *What About Everything?, Another Man's Woman*

THE CARS

These guys began in Boston, Massachusetts, in 1976. By 1978, they were voted Best New Artist in a *Rolling Stone* reader's poll. By 1984, they were on top of the world as recipients of the first ever

MTV Music Video Award for Video Of The Year. (For their single "You Might Think.")

They chose the name The Cars because the automobile was the symbol of teenage spirit and nightlife. That's the image the band wanted to create. A blend of fifties revival, pop/punk, and a ton of new wave style synthesizers make this band one of the first to require a term like "genre-bending".

Signature songs: *Just What I Needed, You Might Think*
Insight song: *Hello Again*

CHEAP TRICK

This rock band formed in Rockford, Illinois, in 1973, and first achieved success with the American mainstream in 1979. However, they did so with the live version of "I Want You To Want Me." This song was recorded in Japan along with everything else on *Cheap Trick At Budokan*. This was because Cheap Trick was somewhat famous in Japan by then. In fact, they first started getting attention there in 1977. (I wonder how long it took these guys to see *Star Wars*.)

They got the idea for their band name at a concert when Slade bassist, Tom Peterson, told the crowd, "We've used every cheap trick in the book…"

Signature songs: *I Want You To Want Me, The Flame, Don't Be Cruel (*Cover*)*
Insight song: *She's Tight*

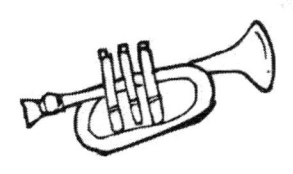

CHERRY POPPIN' DADDIES

This band wanted something that would get them noticed and previous names, like Big Yank and Mr. Wiggles, weren't cutting it, even in Eugene, Oregon.

Lead singer, Steve Perry, claims to have chosen the name from an old R&B record. Their edgy lyrics mixed with big band style created something new; alternative swing, if you will. When swing made its resurgence in the late nineties, they sold two million copies of their compilation album, *Zoot Suit Riot*.

Signature song: *Zoot Suit Riot*
Insight song: *Drunk Daddy*

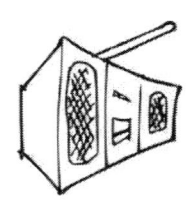

CHICAGO

Although they were indeed from Chicago, Illinois, the band started out as The Big Thing. It was their manager and producer, James Guercio, who convinced them to change it to Chicago Transit Authority. They shortened it to Chicago when the City threatened to sue.

Veterans of the classic rock era, they have dozens of hits with a style that supports the vocals of their lead singer, Peter Cetera, who sounds a lot like Sting.

Signature songs: *Saturday In The Park, If You Leave Me Now, Look Away*
Insight song: *Along Comes a Woman*

CHUMBAWAMBA

In 1982, four musicians from a Burnley, England, band called Chimp Eats Banana moved to the town of Armly, which is west of Leeds. Calling themselves Skin Disease for a compilation EP, and adding more members, they kept changing their sound and their name.

As the story goes, Boff Whalley, lead guitarist, had a dream where he was in a place with lots of strange people and strange music. In this dream, he was presented with two bathroom doors. One door said, Chumba, and the other said, Wamba. He put the two together since his band had both Chumbas and Wambas in it.

Chumbawamba's music is as politically charged as their outside activism. However, their sound isn't so gruff. Savvy electro-funk arrangements keep all six band members busy, and good consistent songwriting reveals them as the underrated savants they are.

Signature song: Tubthumbing
Insight songs: A Man Walks Into A Bar, Mary Mary, Just Desserts

CHUNK! NO, CAPTAIN CHUNK!

This Paris, France, band is kind of punk, kind of pop, and kind of hardcore. That means they growl into the mic only every other song. Their name came from the 1985 Steven Spielberg film, *The Goonies*.

Signature song: In Friends We Trust
Insight song: Restart

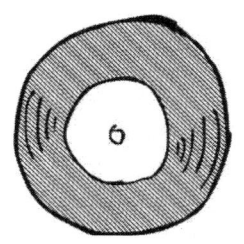

CIRCLE JERKS

Keith Morris left Black Flag to start this band and did all right for himself in the L.A. punk scene of the early eighties. Eventually, he would be regarded as a noted leader in American punk revolution. The name Circle Jerks was chosen for shock value, and with songs like "World Up My Ass" it would need to be a pretty big shock.

Signature songs: *Group Sex, Live Fast Die Young*
Insight songs: *Making the Bombs, World Up My Ass*

THE CLASH

These London punk rockers, once dubbed by CBS Records as "The only band that matters," took their name from a newspaper headline that described a 'clash' with police. A surprisingly small entry for a giant band but, like their music, this one gets right to the point.

Signature songs: *Should I Stay Or Should I Go, London Calling, Train In Vain, Rock The Casbah*
Insight song: *Julie's Been Working For The Drug Squad*

CLUTCH

Possibly the most perfectly named band in this collection. Clutch is always in the pocket with razor timing, and ready to kick it into a higher gear. Their blues rock vibe sounds like the band baby of White Zombie and Lynyrd Skynyrd. That's a lot of great music from Germantown, Maryland.

Fans of bands like Prong and Swiz, they desired a monosyllabic name as well. Neil Fallon, lead singer, rhythm guitarist and keyboardist, doesn't recall who first put Clutch on a poster for an upcoming show, but the name stuck through several gigs. By default, it became the final choice.

Signature song: *Electric Worry*
Insight songs: *A Quick Death In Texas, In Walks Barbarella, We Need Some Money, Pigtown Blues*

COLDPLAY

Originally called Starfish, these London blokes took the name Coldplay from another group when they broke up. The name came from a book of children's poems. I would describe this band's music as pretty mopey for their first few albums, then, beginning with *Mylo Xyloto*, they turned into a much happier sounding band. (This happens to coincide with lead singer Chris Martin's divorce from Gwyneth Paltrow.)

Signature songs: *Yellow, Clocks, Hymn For The Weekend*
Insight songs: *Trouble In Town, Us Against The World, Arabesque, People of the Pride*

CONCRETE BLONDE

This underrated band started out in Hollywood, California, and their name was inspired by R.E.M. front man, Michael Stipe. Stipe described their music as both hard and soft at the same time. "Like a concrete blonde."

Signature songs: *Joey, Everybody Knows*
Insight song: *Dance Along The Edge*

COUNTING CROWS

This band began as a duo in San Francisco and the name was taken from a British nursery rhyme about counting magpies. Known now as "One for Sorrow" the words have been modified over the centuries, but the oldest "newest" version is from the late 1800s:

One for Sorrow
Two for joy
Three for a girl
Four for a boy
Five for silver
Six for gold
Seven for a secret
Never to be told
Eight for a wish
Nine for a kiss
Ten for a bird
You must not miss

Signature songs: *Mr. Jones, A Long December*
Insight songs: *Omaha, Anna Begins*

CRACKER

After disbanding Camper Van Beethoven, David Lowery moved from California to Virginia, and recorded *Big Dirty Yellow Demos* with his childhood friend, Johnny Hickman. It was for fans still mourning the death of his former band, but wound up being the first material for their new band, Cracker. They fancied themselves ultra-white guys, so the name seemed funny. Musically, they have a back porch punk vibe. Not as fast as usual punk, but even more cynical.

Signature song: *Teen Angst*
Insight song: *Happy Birthday To Me*

THE CRANBERRIES

Niall Quinn, original lead singer of this Irish alternative band, named them The Cranberry Saw Us because when the name was said quickly, it would sound like The Cranberry Sauce. Deloris O'Riordan wisely shortened it when she replaced him as lead singer. They sent out demo tapes with the name Cranberry's, but the first one came back addressed to The Cranberries, which they liked better.

Signature songs: *Linger, Zombie*
Insight song: *Salvation*

CREAM

Made up of the finest un-attached rock musicians England had to offer in 1966, this group saw themselves as "the cream of the crop." With Eric Clapton on guitar, Jack Bruce on bass, and Ginger Baker on drums, they weren't wrong. Cream is generally considered to be the first supergroup.

Signature songs: *Sunshine Of Your Love, White Room*
Insight song: *Badge*

CREEDENCE CLEARWATER REVIVAL

This band was once called the Golliwogs, but everyone just had to know it was never going to work. Their new name was borrowed from a few sources. First, was bandleader John Fogerty's friend, Norvel Creedence. Second, was John's favorite beer, Clearwater, which was discontinued but brought back by a different brewery. A Clearwater revival, if you will.

Everything about this band's vibe may feel all swamps and mosquito nets but they're from San Francisco, where psychedelic music was all the rage. (With a fair amount of folk music. It was the sixties, after all.)

Signature songs: *Proud Mary, Bad Moon Rising*
Insight song: *Born On The Bayou*

THE CRICKETS
Buddy Holly was already a star in his hometown of Lubbock, Texas, and was trying to record "That'll Be the Day" but still had contract obligations with Decca Records. His producer, Norman Petty, suggested choosing a band name for the trio with hopes that Decca wouldn't recognize Buddy's voice. The fellas were interested in choosing an insect name and even considered calling themselves The Beetles. (This would be in 1957, way before anyone ever heard of The Beatles including The Beatles.) Bass player, Jerry Allison, suggested crickets because they were "critters known for making music."
Signature songs: *That'll Be The Day, Peggy Sue*
Insight song: *Think it Over*

THE CRYSTAL METHOD
This band is another rock 'n' roll pun. Meant indeed to sound like crystal meth, which was a big deal back in the nineties, as evidenced by the fact that they were calling it crystal meth, and not just meth. I mean, I get that there's an actual difference, but back then all meth was crystal meth, and it was the lead story on more than a few national news broadcasts.

One might think that this would be a rather gritty name for an electro duo but, as that genre goes, these guys earned it with a thoroughly badass sound.

They named their debut album after their hometown of Vegas, and it became a pioneer in dance music and went

platinum. That's one million albums sold in 1997 alone. Which is a lot for bleep-blorp music, even back when bleep-blorp music was all the rage. (I have it on vinyl.)
Signature songs: *Busy Child, Trip Like I Do*
Insight song: *Name Of The Game*

THE CURE
Like other bands in this book, The Cure took their name from an early song of theirs. In this case, the song was called "Easy Cure." As they were honing their sound from Crawly, England, in 1976, front man Robert Smith felt that Easy Cure was too "American sounding". So, he called his band The Cure instead.

Most would agree that this is the band that broke the dam, ushering in a wave of emo music from England.

Signature songs: *Pictures Of You, Lovesong, Friday I'm in Love*
Insight song: *Just Like Heaven*

D

DAFT PUNK
This Paris duo took their name from a poor review of their previous band's single "Cindy So Loud." The columnist, Dave Jennings, described the song as "daft punk thrash." When that band dissolved, Thomas Bangalter and bandmate Guy-Manuel de Homen-Christo, used the jibe as their new band's name.
Signature songs: *Around The World, Get Lucky*
Insight song: *Instant Crush*

DEAD BOYS
It's about time a band from Cleveland, Ohio, made an appearance in this book! Punk music legends everywhere cite Dead Boys as an inspiration despite their short career, which only produced two studio albums. Dead Boys came partly from another legendary band in Cleveland called Rocket From the Tombs. Who else would come out of tombs but a bunch of Dead Boys?
Signature song: *Sonic Reducer*
Insight song: *Caught With The Meat In Your Mouth*

DEAD KENNEDYS

We've all learned by now that punk bands are known for names that evoke emotion or, better yet, produce shock. While this name certainly carries on that tradition, the meaning behind Dead Kennedys is even more depressing than their crude reminder of two assassinations that still felt fresh when the band formed in 1978. Lead singer, Jello Biafra, has often said that the band name was, in fact, their way of documenting the death of the American dream itself.

Signature song: *Holiday In Cambodia*
Insight song: *Police Truck*

THE DEAD MILKMEN

Philadelphia, Pennsylvania, is a very interesting city musically. It produces bands of all varieties. Many cities do, of course, but Philly stretches the spectrum. From hip-hop to punk, take note of the bands that come from this jam town.

The Dead Milkmen play the kind of punk music that even girls could like. It's as silly lyrically as it is haphazardly arranged. Which is to say, you can hear the silly lyrics. In 1985, The Dead Milkmen made a splash with "Bitchin' Camaro" from their debut album, *Big Lizard In My Back Yard*. Three years later, they had a bona fide hit with "Punk Rock Girl" from their third album, *Beelzebubba*. This is funny to me because I prefer the album that sits in between the two, a wild ride called *Bucky Fellini*.

Since my next two books in this series will focus on both sophomore albums and regions of rock, respectively, The Dead Milkmen, and Philadelphia, will certainly be further explored.

The band took their name from the 1977 Toni Morrison novel, *Song of Solomon*. The main character, Malcom Dead III, is nicknamed Milkman.

Signature songs: *Instant Club Hit (You'll Dance To Anything), Punk Rock Girl, Bitchin' Camaro*

Insight songs: *Jellyfish Heaven, Stuart, The Infant Of Prague Customized My Van, Moron, Peter Bazooka, I Dream Of Jesus, Now I Wanna Hold Your Dog, The Thing That Only Eats Hippies, Nitro Burning Funny Cars, The Conspiracy Song, Smokin' Banana Peels*

DEADMAU5

Canadian musician and producer Joel Thomas Zimmerman once had a computer start smoking. A dead mouse inside was found to be the cause. He used the name in various chat rooms for a while and later as a name for his DJ persona. He uses a German spelling structure, which always makes me think of Bauhaus. You will also notice that he substitutes the number 5 for the letter *s*.

Signature song: *Strobe*
Insight song: *The Veldt*

DEATH CAB FOR CUTIE

These guys are from Bellingham, Washington, which sits between Seattle and Vancouver. That whole area has been a hotbed of rock.

This band was originally a solo project for singer/songwriter, Ben Gibbard, who got himself a record deal and then decided to expand his vision, which included adding three more musicians who all play multiple instruments. The band has three guitar players and three keyboard players. Just think about the possibilities!

They took their name from a song called "Death Cab For Cutie" which was on the album *Gorilla* by Bonzo Dog Do Dah Band. (Now, I definitely have to go back up and create an entry for Bonzo Dog Do Dah Band.) Anyway, that song was also in The Beatles' *Magical Mystery Tour* movie. Not on the soundtrack, mind you, but *in* the movie.

Signature songs: *I Will Possess Your Heart, I Will Follow You Into The Dark*

Insight song: *Meet Me On The Equinox*

THE DEATH SET

When I research each band but can't find a legitimate origin for their name, I usually make one last attempt to contact the record company, PR rep, or even the band themselves. Those endeavors usually fail, so I save them for my Hail Mary before moving on.

As a matter of fact, out of fifteen such personal inquiries, only one band member has ever responded. And it was the one person I never expected.

I found The Death Set in December 2019. I did not know how much I needed an electro-punk band in my life. For a guy like me, who loves The Misfits as much as he loves The Crystal Method, I practically snorted both albums, an EP, and a collection of early singles. Yet, it wasn't enough. The Death Set, despite their gritty name, is a fun, warm, smart, and fearless band that knows how to make a minute feel like half the night.

While researching, I discovered that they originated in Sydney, Australia, but moved to Baltimore, then Philly, and then finally Brooklyn, New York, to find a local audience that shared their vibe. Knowing Brooklyn, I'm not surprised they found their home there. It's a pretty badass borough.

Although I never found a story about their band name, I was saddened to discover that founding band member, Beau Velasco, died suddenly in 2009. The band carried on knowing how important the music was to their friend. When I reached out to the other founding member, Johnny Siera, to ask about the band name, I knew it would require him to have to speak of Beau. Since I was a stranger, sending him an online private message, I would've understood if he wasn't inclined to explore such personal, and perhaps painful, memories.

What I got in response was a warm, witty reply that explained that Beau chose the name because it sounded like a gang patch you could put on your vest. "A set, a squad, a pack," Johnny wrote back.

With his permission, I'm also happy to share this segment from Johnny's response: "As the years have gone by, the name has taken on a different meaning to me. It's become a 'memento mori,' a reminder of our joined mortality and the temporality of this Earthly life; and as such, a reminder to live life to the fullest."

Signature songs: *Negative Thinking, We Are Going Anywhere Man, Can You See Straight?*

Insight songs: *I Miss You Beau Velasco, Michel Poiccard Prefers the Old (She Yearns for the Devil), Best Kept Mess*

THE DECEMBERISTS

This quirky band from Portland, Oregon, got their name from a Russian revolt in 1825. This part of Imperial Russian history is known as the Decembrist Revolt. The group's sound is like a more orchestrated Violent Femmes. Highly lyrical with a tenor on vocals, and enough oddities to create their own circus.

Signature song: *Severed*

Insight song: *The Mariner's Revenge Song*

DEEP PURPLE

It was 1967. The summer of love, if there was such a sentiment in Hertfordshire County, England. The drummer for Searchers, Chris Curtis, had an idea for a band that would rotate members like a roundabout. In fact, that's what he called the band before there even was one. He secured a manager and financial backing, then immediately hired Jon Lord, his flatmate, who could play the hell out of an organ.

Curtis's musical idea worked out well. Roundabout had alternating musicians and commercial success. During a tour through Sweden and Denmark guitarist Richie Blackmore, who once played with The Renegades, suggested Deep Purple as a name. It was his grandmother's favorite song, written by pianist Peter DeRose who performed on NBC radio all through the 1920s and 1930s.

While musing over the name change, the band also considered Concrete God. But, in the end, Deep Purple was chosen because it was the safer of the two. This is funny now considering that along with Black Sabbath and Led Zeppelin, they complete the trinity of unholy British hard rock. Dubbed so by the seventies British press.

Signature songs: *Smoke On The Water, Hush, Woman From Tokyo*

Insight song: *Ted The Mechanic*

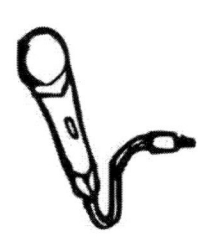

DEPECHE MODE

This was the first band Vince Clarke formed before leaving to create the band Yazoo (Yaz in America) with Allison Moyette, which he then left to create yet another top-ten band, Erasure, with Andy Bell.

They took their name from a French fashion magazine

called *Depeche Mode*. The English translation is Fashion Dispatch, and the band chose this name even though they were from Basildon, England. I guess Bored in Essex was already taken. (Londoners will like that joke.)

Signature songs: *Strangelove, Personal Jesus*
Insight song: *Dangerous*

DER PLAN

This German electronic band isn't as techno as Kraftwerk, nor are they as industrial as Mussolini Headkick, but they deserve credit for advancing the German new wave movement. Their first single "Der Plan" was recorded on cassette in an underground shelter in 1979. They produced 1,500 copies.

They took their name from the 1978 Gordon Rattray Taylor book, *The Biological Time Bomb*. The phrase, der plan, is used to describe what distinguishes humans from animals.

Signature songs: *Der Plan, Ulrike*
Insight song: *Space Bob*

THE DEVIL WEARS PRADA

At best this is an okay band name, until you find out that these guys are a hardcore, Christian band. Now, it's hilarious.

From Dayton, Ohio, they took their name from the 2003 novel by Lauren Weisberger. One might think that they named themselves after the movie, which would still

count, but I try to make the distinction when possible. In this case, the band came before the movie so, obviously, it was the book that inspired the name.
Signature songs: *The Thread, Chemical*
Insight song: *Hey John What's Your Name Again?*

DEVO
Wow! Two Ohio bands in a row! These Ohio boys are actually two sets of brothers. Their name is an abbreviation of de-evolution. Devo was known for their political satire and science-fiction themes with memorable and wacky stage shows.
Signature song: *Whip It*
Insight song: *Mongoloid*

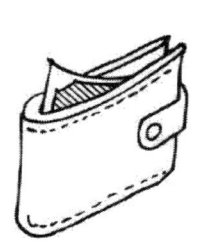

DIRE STRAITS
This band chose a name that described their financial situation as they were putting their rock sound together in London in the late seventies.
Signature songs: *Sultans Of Swing, Money for Nothin'*
Insight song: *Heavy Fuel*

THE DIRTY HEADS
The most successful reggae rock band in a decade, these Huntington Beach, Californians are associated with acts like Sublime and 311. They got their name from something shouted at them as they ran away with a stolen case of beer. "Come back here,

you little dirty heads!"
Signature song: *Cabin By The Sea*
Insight song: *Mongo Push*

THE DISMEMBERMENT PLAN
Also known as D Plan, this Washington, D.C., indie rock group took their name from the Bill Murray film, *Groundhog Day*. Bill's character, Phil Connors, is routinely accosted by insurance salesman, Ned Ryerson, played by Steven Tobolowsky. One of the plans Ned pitches is the dismemberment plan. (Ad-libbed by Tobolowsky.)
Signature song: *Time Bomb*
Insight song: *You Are Invited*

THE DOORS
If you ever listened to The Doors in concert, no doubt you heard their consistent, (and contracted) intro: "From Los Angeles, California, The Doors!" They were proud to be from the epicenter of the sixties counterculture movement. (Even if it was truly almost four hundred miles north in San Francisco.)
The well-known origin of this band name is taken from the Aldous Huxley book, *The Doors of Perception*, which was, in itself, a reference to the William Blake book, *The Marriage of Heaven and Hell*.
Here is the original quote: "If the doors of perception were

cleansed, everything would appear to man, as it is, infinite. For man has closed himself up, so he sees things thro' narrow chinks of his cavern." –William Blake.

The Doors play a blues centered rock with psychedelic elements, especially live. Originally, they searched for a bass player but the music couldn't wait, and they went on without one. Keyboardist, Ray Manzarek, knew he could fill out their sound with his big organ, and he was right. Organ plays as big a part of their music as Jim Morrison's crooning of mystical lyrics.

Side note: After Jim Morrison's death, the band tried to hire Iggy Pop as their new lead singer.

Signature songs: *Break On Through, Light My Fire, People Are Strange, L.A. Woman, Riders On The Storm*
Insight songs: *The Mosquito , The Changeling*

DREAM THEATER

If Pink Floyd and TOOL had a baby, it would be Dream Theater. Their name was taken from the Dream Theater in their hometown of Monterey, California. They had been calling themselves Majesty, which stemmed from a comment about their early song "Bastille Day," but wanted a change. It was (original) drummer Mike Portnoy's father who suggested Dream Theater.

Signature song: *Pull Me Under*
Insight song(s): *In The Presence Of Enemies Parts I & II*

DROPKICK MURPHYS

Named after wrestler John "Dropkick" Murphy. He and his wife ran the Bellows Farm Sanitarium, their home, as an alcoholism treatment center outside of Boston. People referred to it as Dropkick Murphy's.

Signature song: *I'm Shippin' Off To Boston*
Insight song: *Worker's Song*

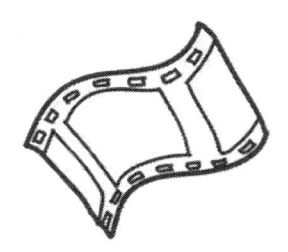

DURAN DURAN

Brit-pop from Birmingham. These blokes formed their band in 1978, but they practically owned the eighties. One might say they were notorious. Like their contemporaries, they spent a lot of time and effort making captivating music videos. Unlike their contemporaries, they shot their videos on 35mm film which gave their productions a more polished look than the rest.

Their name was taken from the 1968 sci-fi film, *Barbarella*, and the antagonist, Durand-Durand, the cunning concierge.

Signature songs: *Notorious, The Reflex, A View To A Kill, Rio, Wild Boys, Girls On Film*
Insight song: *Hold Back The Rain*

E

THE EAGLES
Partly an homage to the Byrds, Don Henley recalls that the group wanted something simple, American, and slightly spiritual. The Eagles sounded a bit like the name of a street gang at first, but it certainly hit all the other marks so they kept it.

Signature songs: *Hotel California, Desperado*
Insight song: *One of These Nights*

EARTH, WIND & FIRE
This group was called the Salty Peppers and signed to Capitol Records, but didn't draw much attention beyond Chicago. When they signed with Warner Bros. Records in the early seventies, they changed their name to reflect the elements. Water being the obvious omission. (That's like naming your kids John, Paul, and George. Sorry, but you owe us another kid. You owe us a Ringo).

Signature song: *Let's Groove*
Insight song: *Sing A Song*

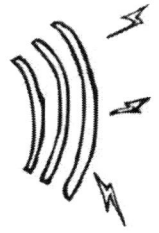

ECHO AND THE BUNNYMEN

The rumor is that their drum machine was nicknamed Echo and The Bunnymen was a pet name for fellow Liverpool band, Frankie Goes To Hollywood. According to guitarist, Will Sergeant, this is all a myth and the name was suggested by a mate who often tossed out funny monikers like The Daz Men or Fan Extractors. The group then chose the one they liked the best. But there are those who maintain that it was, in fact, their drum machine and Frankie Goes To Hollywood that inspired the name.

They achieved their biggest success with a cover of "People Are Strange" which appears on the *Lost Boys* soundtrack.

Signature song: *The Killing Moon*
Insight song: *Lips Like Sugar*

EIFFEL 65

This Italian electronic band wanted something recognizable for their name, something global. Being technology hounds, they used a random word generator and the word Eiffel showed up. According to myth, 6 and 5 were the first two digits in a phone number that their agent mistook for part of the band name, and it stuck.

Signature songs: *Blue, Move Your Body*
Insight songs: *Living In A Bubble, Too Much Of Heaven*

ELECTRIC LIGHT ORCHESTRA

A play on the words electric light, as in electric light bulb, (which appears in their early album art), and electric music with a light orchestral touch. Stringed instruments were all the rage in the sixties, and ELO wanted to emulate that sound. Band founder and only current member, Jeff Lynne, has worked with The Beatles and Tom Petty among many others. He was also a member of the Traveling Wilburys, as both Otis and Clayton Wilbury.

Signature songs: *Telephone Man, Sweet Talkin' Woman*
Insight song: *Do Ya*

EMINEM

Marshal Mathers chose this name because it represents his initials, *M,* and *M*. He spelled it weird because that's what everybody was doing in the nineties. A native of Detroit, Michigan, Eminem is the most successful rapper in RIAA history.

Signature songs: *The Real Slim Shady, Lose Yourself, G.O.A.T., Purple Pills (With D12), My Band (With D12)*
Insight song: *Cleaning Out My Closet*

ERASURE

Remember the guy who left Depeche Mode to form Yaz, and then disbanded Yaz to form Erasure? His name is Vince Clarke, and everything he touches turns to techno gold. When he met Andy Bell, he went platinum.

As the story goes, the two fellows were thinking up band names and writing them down in pencil. The names were erased and written over and over. After a while, they were left with no words but some very obvious erasures.

Signature songs: *Oh L'amour, A Little Respect, Chains of Love, Dead of Night, Knocking On Your Door, Hideway*
Insight songs: *Piano Song, Chorus, Sweet Sweet Baby*

EURYTHMICS

Annie Lennox and David A. Stewart were in a band called The Catch before it broke up and became The Tourists, which also broke up.

They decided to form a duo in Wagga Wagga, Australia, even though their roots were not only from Europe but so was their new chosen name. Eurythmics is a combination of the words, *Europe* and *rhythm*.

Signature songs: *Sweet Dreams, Missionary Man*
Insight song: *Sisters Are Doing It For Themselves*

EVANESCENCE

These explosive Little Rock, Arkansas, musicians chose Evanescence because the band wanted to include a visual artistic component to their music and the mystical sounding name lent to that idea. They also liked the definition of evanescent: *Passing from sight.*

Signature songs: *My Immortal, Bring Me To Life*
Insight song: *Taking Over Me*

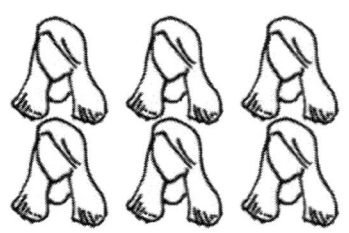

EVE 6

This is a power trio of alternative rockers from Southern California, La Crescenta, to be exact. They formed as Yakoo, then became Eleventeen, and finally settled on Eve 6 in their third year of performing.

That name was taken from a 1993 season one episode of *The X-Files* which had cloned characters named Eve 6, 7, 8, 9, and 10.

Signature songs: *Inside Out, Here's To The Night*
Insight song: *Open Road Song*

EVERYTHING BUT THE GIRL

This duo formed in Kingston Upon Hull, England, by solo artists Tracey Thorn and Ben Watt. They each had record contracts, but formed a band together on the side that explored a jazz/pop sound.

The two musicians were romantically involved and eventually got married, but all in private. Even longtime fans were not aware of their relationship until the band became inactive.

In Hull, there is a furniture store called Turners, and their sales slogan is "Everything But The Girl." The band borrowed it just long enough to earn four top-ten singles, and eight more songs that cracked the Top 40.

Signature songs: *Missing, Driving, Wrong*
Insight song: *Five Fathoms*

EXPLOSIONS IN THE SKY

The band had already formed in Austin, Texas, and were performing under the name Breaker Morant, when a July Fourth fireworks display in 1999 caused drummer Chris Hravsky to remark on the "...explosion in the sky..." The band makes epic music that's orchestral in nature. Their albums sound like film scores to movies somebody really should make.

Signature song: *Your Hand In Mine*
Insight song: *First Breath After Coma*

F

FASTBALL

This Austin based trio started out as Magneto. They had to change their name but not because Marvel Comics threatened to sue, which they didn't. As it turns out, there was a boy band in Mexico named Magneto. They went with Magneto USA for a time as they considered other possibilities for band names. Then they saw a baseball themed porn movie called *Fastball*, and they all lived happily ever after.

Signature song: *The Way*
Insight song: *Out Of My Head*

FATBOY SLIM

This Surrey born Englishman is Quentin Leo Cook, but known more commonly as Norman Quentin Cook. He is a giant in the big beat DJ genre. Cook chose the name Fatboy Slim because it was a contradiction in terms. "I've told so many different lies over the years about it, I can't actually remember the truth. It's just an oxymoron—a word that can't exist. It kind of suits me." A lot of names suit him, because he currently holds the Guinness World Record for most Top 40 hits under different pseudonyms. Here are the ones I know of: (And I'm counting them all as bands in this book!)

Arthur Chubb
Asher D. Slim
Biggie Sims
Cheeky Boy
Chemistry
Chimp McGarvey
Cook Da Bass
Disque Attack
DJ Delight
DJ Mega-Mix
DJ Quentox
Drunk Soul Brother
The Feelgood Factor
Fried Funk Food
Grime Minister
Hot Sause 63
Margret Scratcher
Mighty Gus Poyets
Pierre Burner Down
Rockaway Three
Rok Da Radio
Sensateria
Son of Cheeky Boy
Son of Wilmot
Stomping Pondfrogs
Sunny Side Up
Yum Yum Head Food

Signature songs: *Praise You, Rockafeller Skank*
Insight songs: *Brimful Of Asha, Funk Soul Brother*

FEAR AND LOATHING IN LAS VEGAS This band is not from Las Vegas, Nevada, and I can't decide if that comes as a surprise or not. Either way, they're a hardcore/electronic sextet from Kobe, Japan. A rare mash-up of musicality, but these guys pull it off. Both genres are represented fearlessly in each song, and the mixture is not the orange juice and toothpaste taste one would expect. Instead, it's like dipping a slice of green apple in caramel.

In the summer of 2008, two bands, Blank Time and Ending For A Start, morphed into one. Their name is the title of Hunter S. Thompson's 1971 novel. However, it may well be the book's subtitle, *A Savage Journey to the Heart of the American Dream*, that attracted this band's attention.

Signature songs: *Evolution (Entering The New World), Return To Zero*
Insight song: *The Gong Of Knockout*

FINE YOUNG CANABALS Guitarist Dave Cox, and bassist David Steele were in a London band called The Beat. The English Beat, in America. Unbeknownst to them, their bandmates formed a new group, General Public, behind their backs. The band's accountant telephoned Cox and Steele to break the news that The Beat was dissolved.

The two ousted musicians stuck together, and after an

exhaustive search for a strong vocalist that took over five hundred auditions, they had made no offers. Instead, they tracked down an old classmate, Roland Gift, who they knew to be a gifted singer as well as a charismatic front man. They found him singing for a pub band called The Bones and asked him to join their ranks instead. He did, but at least he let his other band down easy.

They took their name from the 1960 film *Fine Young Cannibals*, staring Robert Wagner and Natalie Wood. Also, they won Best Band and Best Album at the 1990 Brit Awards for their sophomore and final album, *The Raw And The Cooked*. After that, Roland went off to pursue a film career that never took off. You know what else never took off? General Public.

Signature song: *She Drives Me Crazy*
Insight song: *Don't Look Back*

FISHBONE

It should be a pretty straightforward story - two brothers with the last name Fisher, one of whom was simply called Fish by friends. But it's not that simple. These funk/ska/punk brothers met more like-minded musicians at school in Los Angeles. By 1979, they had a full band assembled. Six members strong. They chose the name Megatron at first but settled on Fishbone, partly because the word fish was a prominent fixture in their lives. Fishbone sounded funky and dirty, just like their music. They even have a trumpet player known as "Dirty" Walter.

Signature songs: *Everyday Sunday, Ma and Pa*
Insight song: *Freddy's Dead*

FIVE FINGER DEATH PUNCH

From Las Vegas, this hardcore band has some of the best album covers in the business. Their name is a reference to the kung fu quivering palm technique known as *dim mak*, or *touch of death;* a lethal blow using seemingly non-lethal force, likely the result of pressure points, and a well-guarded secret in Chinese fiction. Quentin Tarantino used a similar mythology in *Kill Bill: Vol. 2*, and it was also used in *Kung-Fu Panda, Doctor Who, The Men Who Stare At Goats*, and even in a 1977 episode of the TV show, *Quincy M.E.*

Signature songs: *Wrong Side Of Heaven, Gone Away, Jekyll And Hyde*
Insight song: *Living The Dream*

FLEETWOOD MAC

This band's name is a mash-up of the last names of drummer Mick Fleetwood and bassist John McVie. The other two original members were guitarists Peter Green and Jeremy Spencer. Christine Perfect was a session musician on their sophomore album, *Mr. Wonderful*. She was asked back to contribute to album number three, *Then Play On*. A romance bloomed between her and John, and they married in 1970. She officially joined Fleetwood Mac with the release of their fourth album, *Kiln House*.

Fast forward five albums or so, one of which had a half-monkey, half-elephant on the cover. It was a wild ride but not the success they desired. They were recording in L.A., which was designed to be a fun and fresh experience for the English band. It turned out to be all that, and so much more, when they met Lindsey Buckingham. Before leaving the States, they knew recruiting him was the key to commercial success. Buckingham agreed, with the condition that his bandmate, Stevie Nicks, also be asked to join.

Their eponymous album, 1975's *Fleetwood Mac*, was the first album with the modern line-up, and the most successful produced to date. Their next album, *Rumors*, was no slouch and would set into motion a career that sold more vinyl than all the sex shops in Hollywood combined.

Signature songs: *Don't Stop, Go Your Own Way, Landslide, Little Lies*

Insight song: *Big Love (Live)*

FLOGGING MOLLY

This is the only other Celtic punk band in this book and, like Dropkick Murphys, their name comes from a location combined with a real name. Los Angeles is home to this seven-piece unit, and they played every Monday night at an Irish bar called Molly Malone's. It is said that lead singer, David King, likened

the monotony to flogging a dead horse, and a band name was born.
Signature song: *Devil's Dance Floor*
Insight song: *If I Ever Leave This World Alive*

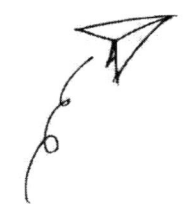

FOO FIGHTERS
This Seattle band was formed by former Nirvana drummer, Dave Grohl, after the suicide of lead singer Kurt Cobain. The term "foo" was used in WWII to describe aerial debris, UFOs, or any other anomalous phenomena. The phrase was coined by the 415th Night Fighter Squadron in November 1944. Pilots, many of which believed foo fighters were deployed by the enemy, used the term to report anything they couldn't explain.
Signature songs: *Everlong, Best Of You, My Hero*
Insight song: *Learn To Fly*

FOREIGNER
Mick Jones (not the Mick Jones from The Clash) started this band in New York City. Already a famed guitarist from England, he chose the name Foreigner because that's what he was, and that's how he felt.
Signature songs: *Hot Blooded, Urgent, Cold As Ice*
Insight song: *Say You Will*

FOSTER THE PEOPLE

When Foster *and* the People were getting their start in Los Angeles they were frequently introduced as Foster the People. Band founder Mark Foster and his bandmates thought that sounded cooler.

Signature song: *Pumped Up Kicks*
Insight song: *Are You What You Want To Be?*

FOUNTAINS OF WAYNE

Two talented musicians, Adam Schlesinger and Chris Collingwood, met at Williams College in Massachusetts. They played together, then went their separate ways, one to Boston, and one to New York City. Then, they got back together and formed a band named after a lawn ornament store in Wayne, New Jersey. Their brand of witty indie rock needed a name like just like this. Previous considerations included Are You My Mother?, Woolly Mammoth, and Three Men Who When Standing Side by Side Have a Wingspan of Over Twelve Feet.

They auditioned drummers by having them play "Swing Town" by The Steve Miller Band.

Signature songs: *Stacy's Mom, Someone To Love, Traffic And Weather*
Insight songs: *Hey Julie, Peace And Love*

THE FOUR SEASONS

Frankie Valli and Bob Gaudio chose the name Four Seasons after the bowling alley in Union Township, New Jersey, where they failed an audition in 1960. They are also known as Frankie Valli and the Four Seasons, but the legal name of the group is Four Seasons Partnership. Along with The Beach Boys, The Four Seasons were the only other American band that maintained commercial success before, during, and after the British invasion of the late sixties and seventies. Both bands were harmony driven, but the Four Seasons has more soul and less sand.

Signature songs: *Earth Angel, Big Girls Don't Cry, Walk Like A Man*
Insight song: *Let's Hang On*

FRANKIE GOES TO HOLLYWOOD

According to Holly Johnson, this Liverpool band was already recording and needed a name so they could book gigs. There was a newspaper article about Frank Sinatra filming a movie and the headline read, 'Frankie Goes to Hollywood'. Boom! Band name.

Signature song: *Relax*
Insight song: *Two Tribes*

THE FRATELLIS

Here is another band that took their name from the Spielberg film, *The Goonies*. It was the Fratelli family who chased the kids through the guts of Astoria, Oregon.

This band comes from Glasgow, Scotland, and play indie rock that sometimes has a comical skew. Not unlike Bowling For Soup, Weezer, or Fountains of Wayne.

Signature songs: *Chelsea Dagger, Whistle For The Choir*
Insight song: *Stand Up Tragedy*

THE FUGS

This band was formed by two poets and a drummer in New York City in 1964. Their first release, *The Village Fugs Sing Ballads of Contemporary Protest, Point of Views, and General Dissatisfaction*, showcased a deadpan folk style, but with lyrics lewd enough to make Frank Zappa blush.

Their name comes from Norman Mailer's 1948 novel *The Naked and the Dead* where, in the American edition, the word *fuck* was replaced with *fug*.

Signature songs: *CIA Man, Kill For Peace, Coca Cola Douche*
Insight song: *Boobs A Lot*

G

GENESIS

This British group was recording their first album, *From Genesis to Revelation*, when their manager suggested Genesis as the name of the new band with a fresh sound.

When Peter Gabriel left to pursue a solo career, the rest of the band recorded demos for the next album and held auditions for a new lead singer. Phil Collins, the drummer, recorded a vocal track. After every audition, the other band members kept saying the same thing, "It was good, but Phil was better." They really had to persuade Phil to take a legitimate run at the song "Squonk," but the result confirmed that the band could carry on without Gabriel and without sacrificing the high level of music they produced.

They recorded *A Trick Of The Tail* with Collins as lead vocalist and then hired drummer Bill Bruford, founding member of Yes, to play on their tour.

Signature songs: *Land Of Confusion, I Can't Dance*
Insight songs: *The Carpet Crawlers, Dreaming While You Sleep, Firth Of Firth*

THE GEORGIA SATELLITES

Indeed from Georgia, these southern rockers played every Monday night in the uptown Atlanta neighborhood of Buckhead. Their original band name was Keith and the Satellites but, when they recorded their first demo, they changed their name to The Georgia Satellites.
Signature songs: *Keep Your Hands To Yourself, Hippie Hippie Shake*
Insight song: *Hard Luck Boy*

GIN BLOSSOMS

The term "gin blossoms" was commonly associated with the reddened face of drunkards, although it's actually a rude euphemism for the skin condition of rosacea. The infamously erroneous book *Hollywood Babylon* by Kenneth Anger includes a picture of W. C. Fields, who suffered from the ailment, along with a caption that reads, "W. C. Fields with gin blossoms."
This indie rock band has an acoustic feel, like Hootie and the Blowfish only a bit darker thematically. They began in Tempe, Arizona, and found fame with their sophomore album, *New Miserable Experience*. Life would imitate art when the band's lead guitarist and primary songwriter, Doug Hopkins, grew more and more depressed. He chose alcohol as his doomed coping mechanism, but his bandmates were reluctant to remove him from the band.

He was a friend and wrote wonderful, woeful music.

A&M Records stepped in and withheld fifteen thousand dollars they owed Hopkins until he signed over half his publishing royalties and agreed to quit the band. He needed the money badly and accepted their offer, which also surrendered one hundred percent of his mechanical royalties. The breakout success of the album, and his song "Hey Jealousy", ended up costing him millions and isolated Hopkins from his bandmates, who went on a worldwide tour.

His suicide in late 1993 was taken hard by the band, but I'm sure A&M put out a heartfelt press release on the nicest glossy paper money could buy.

Signature songs: *Hey Jealousy, Found Out About You*
Insight song: *Lost Horizons*

GNARLS BARKLEY

This duo is made up of Atlanta, Georgia, singer/songwriter Cee-lo Green and White Plains, New York, singer/songwriter Danger Mouse. They obviously intended for the name to sound like Charles Barkley, the famed basketball player, and avoided any legal entanglements by altering it just enough. Legend has it that the final decision was made during a dinner at iHop with napkins used to brainstorm.

Signature songs: *Crazy, Charity Case*
Insight songs: *Storm Coming, Smiley Faces*

GOLDFINGER

Los Angeles has its fair share of ska bands, but this one helped kick off a new wave of popularity in the reggae/punk inspired genre. The group is also known for promoting animal rights. Their name was taken from the 1964 James Bond film of the same name.

Signature songs: *Here In Your Bedroom, Superman*
Insight song: *Wallflower*

GOOD CHARLOTTE

Twin brothers Joel and Benji Madden formed Good Charlotte in Waldorf, Maryland, after attending a Beastie Boys concert in 1995. They recruited a drummer and bass player but their fifth member, a second guitarist, wasn't added until two years later. Billy Martin was in another band but went to one of their shows, was deeply impressed, and bonded with the brothers over their mutual love of the Australian band, Silverchair.

When Joel and Benji were evicted from their apartment, Billy let them move in with him. It was the least they could do to let him join their band after his broke up.

Their band name was taken from the 1969 Carol Beach York book, *Good Charlotte: Girls of the Good Day Orphanage.*

Signature songs: *I just Wanna Live, Lifestyles Of The Rich And Famous*
Insight song: *Last December*

GORILLAZ

This band is considered to be the first, and certainly the most successful, virtual band. Which is to say that although the music is, of course, performed by three real people, the band is presented as an animated line-up of four fictional characters. Damon Albarn, formerly of Blur, founded Gorillaz with artist Jamie Hewlett and have since added Remi Kabaka Jr. as the band's official drummer and producer.

Albarn chose the name Gorillaz for two reasons. One was that it was an homage to the world's first manufactured band, The Monkees (complete with irregular spelling). The other story is that he named the band after a comment made by Liam Gallagher of Oasis. In a radio interview, Liam was asked about his rivalry with fellow London band, Blur. The bands were then compared to the friendly rivalry between The Rolling Stones and The Beatles. Liam was asked if his band would be The Beatles or The Stones. His response was reportedly that Oasis was The Beatles and that Blur was The (fuckin') Monkees! The name Gorillaz is believed to be a nod to that observation.

Signature songs: *Feel Good Inc., Clint Eastwood*
Insight song: *19-2000*

GODSMACK

Sully Erna had been playing drums for almost twenty-five years in Boston bands when he decided to start a new hard rock group, this time as lead singer. The Scam was their original name but, one night, Sully was making fun of a kid in the audience with a cold sore on his lip. The very next day he had one himself. Someone told him it was his Godsmack, then explained that it was a synonymous term for Karma. He loved it.
Signature songs: *Voodoo, I Stand Alone, Awake*
Insight song: *1000hp*

GOLDEN EARRING

Once The Tornados, this progressive Netherlands rock band found themselves as the opening and closing act of a British band called The Hunters. One of their songs, an instrumental piece called "Golden Earrings" gave the boys from the Dutch town of The Hague their name. They dropped the *s* in 1969.
Signature songs: *Radar Love, Twilight Zone*
Insight song: *She Flies On Strange Wings*

GOO GOO DOLLS

Hard to believe this Buffalo, New York, band didn't do better with their first name, Sex Maggots. As the story goes, a promoter refused to book them until they changed it. They found the new name on the back of an old *True Detective* magazine. The name fits their sensible sound better, although hardly a home run, and possibly why this talented group doesn't get more attention outside the monstrous success of "Iris." Along with Sarah McLachlan, they *owned* the *City Of Angels* soundtrack.
Signature song: *Iris*
Insight song: *Black Balloon*

GRAND FUNK RAILROAD

The seventies rock scene will always include this crowd pleasing band. The name is a play on words from the Grand Trunk Western Railroad that ran through their hometown of Flint, Michigan.
Signature songs: *We're an American Band, Some Kind of Wonderful*
Insight songs: *Time Machine, Footstompin' Music*

GRATEFUL DEAD

Godfathers of the jam band, these San Francisco counter-culturalists started out as The Warlocks. But as luck would have it, there was already a local band with the same name. Now you get to hear a story. There is an old English proverb, about a man who enters a village whose residents are fighting over the debts of a dead man. To make matters worse, nobody wants to pay the additional expense of his burial and he has started to sour the air. The newcomer pays for the funeral and even pays off the dead man's debts before moving on with his travels. Later, he is saved by a mystical event that he attributes to "grateful spirits." The band name is their attempt to honor the concept of such grateful spirits.

Signature songs: *Friend Of The Devil, St. Stephen*
Insight song: *Uncle John's Band*

GREEN APPLE QUICKSTEP

This Tacoma, Washington, based band used to play as Inspector Luv and the Ride Me Babys, but changed their name from a song on the 1971 Byrds album, *Byrdmanix*. It should also be noted that the "Green Apple Quickstep" is an old-timey term for the little dance people do when they really have to go to the bathroom, which is exactly what that Byrds song is about.

Interestingly, before Mookie Baylock became Pearl Jam, they played their first show ever show as the opening act

for Inspector Luv and the Ride Me Babys. This was in October 1990 at the Off Ramp Café.
Signature song: *Dizzy*
Insight song: *Bottle*

GREEN DAY

Once known as Sweet Children, the title of an early song, Billy Joe Armstrong chose another early song title to avoid confusion with a similarly named Berkeley, California, band. A Green Day, by the way, was a day where there was plenty of weed.

The band plays power/punk music and hit the big time with their third album, *Dookie*. Their follow-up, *Insomnia*, suffered from sophomore syndrome, even though it was their fourth release.

Signature songs: *Longview, Basket Case, 21 Guns, When September Ends, American Idiot*
Insight songs: *Paper Lanterns, Still Breathing*

GREEN RIVER

Pioneers of the grunge scene in Seattle, this band eventually split. From its ashes sprang two new bands, Pearl Jam and Mudhoney. They took their name from the moniker given to a serial killer active in the Pacific Northwest at the time of their formation. He was called the Green River Killer.

Signature song: *Hangin' Tree*
Insight song: *Rehab Doll*

GUNS N' ROSES

While he was living with L.A. Guns guitarist Tracii Guns, Izzy Stradlin was in his own band with Axl Rose called Hollywood Rose. Guns mentioned to Izzy that his band was in the market for a new lead singer and Izzy suggested Axl, even though it would mean the breakup of his own group. Which it did.

They considered starting their own record company to disperse singles and named the venture Guns N' Roses, a combination of the two disbanded acts.

The record company idea fizzled, but they kept the name to re-launch the band with Izzy on guitar. A few months later, Tracii and Axl got into an argument and he was replaced with Slash.

Signature songs: *Welcome To The Jungle, Paradise City, Sweet Child O' Mine, November Rain, You Could Be Mine*
Insight songs: *Locomotive, Dust And Bones*

FRINGE FARM SUB-SECTION

And now, guest archivist, good friend, and musician Chris Reid will present us with a baker's dozen band names that mainstream music may have forgotten:

AMANAZ

Hailing from Lusaka, Zambia, in Southern Africa, AMANAZ comes from an acronym cooked up by singer/percussionist Keith Kabwe: Ask Me About Nice Artists in Zambia. Early adaptors of what became known as Zamrock—heavily influenced by Deep Purple, the Stones, Grand Funk, and Congolese rumba maestro Franco. All mixed together with a uniquely African point of view.

Signature songs: *Amanaz, Making The Scene*
Insight song: *History Of Man*

THE ASTEROID No. 4

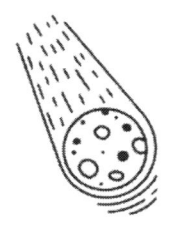

Originally hailing from Psychedelphia—er—Philadelphia, and currently residing in the Bay Area of California, these Spaceman 3 fans thought Asteroid 4 was a little too on the money, so they added a "The," and a number sign (sometimes "#" and sometimes "No.") shortly before they pressed their first single.

They've done trippy stuff, straightforward rock, and even have a country album under their belt.
Signature song: Wicked Wire
Insight songs: Let It Go, As Soon As Dawn, King Richard

CURRENT 93
Led by one-time member of Phychic TV, David Tibet, this sometimes post-industrial, sometimes post-apocalyptic folk, sometimes creepy soundscape, gets its name from Aleister Crowley's "93 Current" of Thelema/Agape. Using a Greek technique, isopsephy, or adding up the numerical value of each letter, Thelma (Will), and Agape (Love), each add up to 93. "Love is the law, love under Will."
Signature songs: Soft Black Stars, The Decent Of Long Satan and Babylon, I Have A Special Plan For This World
Insight songs: Lucifer Over London, Gothic Love Song, Black Ships At The Sky

EINSTRÜZENDE NEUBAUTEN
In Germany, pre-World War II architecture is known as altbauten (old buildings). Those built after the war are known as Neubauten (new buildings). Einstürzen is the verb, to collapse. Hence, their name translated is, Collapsing New Buildings. An early version of the band played their first concert on April Fool's Day 1980, at West Berlin's Moon Club.

Signature song: *Yu-Gung*
Insight song: *Headcleaner*

GERMAN OAK

Until recently re-issued by Now-Again Records, German Oak was a mysterious exoteric German band whose album was highly sought after on the collector's market. They were originally called Reaktor but, when they decided to change musical directions, they also wanted a new name.

German Oak came to them while rehearsing in a WWII era bunker in Düsseldorf-Hamm. Their manager jumped on it and released the rehearsal tapes as an album under that name.

Signature song*: Bella's Song*
Insight song*: Nothing Bear Song*

HÜSKER DÜ

The greatest band to come from St. Paul, Minnesota, got their name when bassist Greg Norton and drummer Grant Hart were listening to "Psycho Killer" by The Talking Heads. Rather than singing, "Psycho killer qu'est-ce que, c'est" they hollered, "Husker Du!" a Danish and Norwegian phrase meaning, "Do you remember?" Also, the name of a seventies era board game.

They added the umlauts over the *u* to make it look more metal.

Signature song: *Eight Miles High*
Insight songs: *Celebrated Summer, In A Free Land, Hardly Getting Over It*

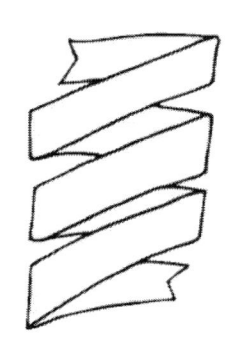

SISTERS OF MERCY

What do you get when you cross Leonard Cohen, Motorhead, Suicide, and the Stooges? I'm not sure, but there is a band that formed in Leeds in 1979 that gave it their best try. The band name comes from a song featured in the movie *McCabe and Mrs. Miller*. Or from the order of Catholic Nuns.

Signature song: *This Corrosion*
Insight songs: *Alice, Ribbons*

THE SOFT BOYS

The band where Robyn Hitchcock first made his mark. He tells their story, including how they got their name in this lengthy quote. "I pictured the Soft Boys a bit like civil servants. They were powerful, but you wouldn't see them. They were invisible, but they had a huge influence. Funnily enough, that's kind of what happened. My vision of them was that they had been filtered; they had no bones so they could slide under doors and then come back up, like in the *Terminator* movies, so they could get anywhere, through a keyhole or under a door. They would be bloodless, like they had been drained like Halal, but they would be alive. They didn't have bones, and they also had a tremendous sexual appetite in some ghastly way that was left to the imagination. I thought, this is too good, so I had to write about it in a song and came up with 'Give it to the Soft Boys.' We were also in one sense very soft. We were middle class, mother's boys, wouldn't hurt a fly, couldn't confront anyone, never mind each other, very nice people who avoided eye contact and really liked Monty Python and kind of laughing at things quietly in silent laughter. Anyway, there it was in a way. We did become invisible, but an influential force after our demise."

Signature song: *Give It To The Soft Boys*
Insight songs: *Queen of Eyes, Tonight, I Wanna Destroy You*

THE SOFT MACHINE

Germinating from the seeds of a band called Wilde Flowers, The Soft Machine pioneered psychedelic-progressive-jazz-rock-fusion in the heart of Canterbury, England. Their sound became known as the Canterbury sound. Passing through its ranks were luminaries such as Robert Wyatt, Kevin Ayers, Daevid Allen, and Mike Ratledge.

The band's name comes from the title of the first novel in William S. Burroughs's Nova Trilogy.

Signature songs: *Hope for Happiness, Why Are We Sleeping?*
Insight song: *Rivmic Melodies*

SPACEMEN 3

Coming together in the early eighties in Rugby, England, this band of outsiders were originally The Spacemen, owing to the fact that they felt alien to their local scene. An early gig flier featured a large unrelated 3 on the poster. The poster was titled, Are Your Dreams At Night 3 Sizes Too Big? But the layout made it look like the band was called The Spacemen 3. Never mind the fact that there were four people in the band.

The 3 was adopted, but the "The" was dropped because it now reminded them too much of a fifties rock 'n' roll, or sixties surf band.

Signature song: Revolution
Insight songs: Transparent Radiation, OD Catastrophe, Honey

SYMARIP

Originally known as The Bees, Symarip got their name when they were ready to release an album but were under contract to another label as The Pyramids. They reversed the word pyramids, then changed a few letters around. Generally considered to be the first skinhead reggae band, as they targeted the early skinheads as their audience.

Signature song: Skinhead Moonstomp
Insight songs: Skinflint, Skinhead Jamboree

THEE MICHELLE GUN ELEPHANT

According to lead singer Yusuke Chiba this Japanese band got their name from their bass player who saw a copy of *Machine Gun Etiqutte* by The Dammed in Chiba's record collection and asked, "What the hell is this Michelle Gun Elephant?"

"Thee" was taken from a long line of eighties garage rock bands spearheaded by Thee Headcoats. Or if we want to go all the way back to the Sixties, Thee Midnighters.

Signature song: *GWD*
Insight songs: *West Cabaret Drive, Deadman's Galaxy Days, Plasma Drive*

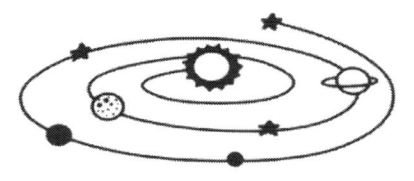

WOODEN SHJIPS

This San Francisco motorik drone band named themselves after a Jefferson Airplane song. They added a *j* to ships to make them sound Swedish and give them a California/Scandinavian vibe. And made them easier to find on the Internet.

Signature song: *We Ask You To Ride*
Insight songs: *For So Long, Back To Land*

H

HARD-FI

These guys are from England, in a town called Stains-Upon-Thames. (Not pronounced stains, but stans). They were admirers of legendary reggae dub musician and producer Lee "Scratch" Perry whose sound was christened as "Hard-Fi". As opposed to the term "Hi-Fi" which stands for High Fidelity. They named their band after this term as an homage to Lee.

Signature songs: *Cash Machine, Better Do Better, Gotta Reason*
Insight songs: *I Shall Overcome, Killer Sounds*

HAWTHORNE HEIGHTS

Named after the author Nathaniel Hawthorne, this five piece Dayton band first formed in 2001 as A Day In The Life; named after the last song on *Sgt. Pepper's Lonely Hearts Club Band*, and The Beatles' contribution to the famed 1967 Summer of Love. Hawthorne Heights performed and recorded under that name for two years. Bassist Matt Ridenour, inspired by the Hawthorn Inn & Suites on his daily walk to work, suggested the regal sounding Hawthorne Heights as a replacement in 2003. The rest of the band agreed and promptly released two certified gold albums.

In 2007 the musicians tragically lost their rhythm guitarist, and friend, Casey Calvert. Casey was taking anti-seizure and anti-depression medication, but did not exceed the prescribed dosage. His death was ruled an accident.

The band used each other, and their art, to cope with the loss of their friend. They were just one day into a new tour to promote their sophomore album, *If Only You Were Lonely*. The songs "Four Became One" and "Sugar In The Engine" are dedicated to Casey on their first album without him, 2008's *Fragile Future*.

Signature songs: *Ohio Is For Lovers, Saying Sorry*
Insight songs: *Hard To Breathe, Sugar In The Engine*

HEART

The long history of this Seattle area band involves several name changes and line-up shuffles. The oldest version of the group, known as The Army, was created in 1967. Two years later came the first personnel and name change. The band became White Heart, inspired by *Tales From White Heart* by Arthur C. Clarke. They even asked for and received permission to use the name.

As they were getting ready to release their debut album on Valentine's Day 1970, which was also founding member Roger Fisher's birthday, they decided to shorten their name to Heart. They went through another member change in 1971 when Ann Wilson joined the band, and they renamed themselves, Hocus Pocus.

Roger Fisher's brother, Mike, was the band's sound engineer but fled to Canada to avoid the draft. Sometimes he would sneak back across the border to assist the band. On one of these trips, he and Ann Wilson became romantically involved and fell in love. She followed him back to Vancouver and, shortly after, the rest of the band did the same. The group also gained Ann's sister, Nancy Wilson, who, in true Fleetwood Mac fashion, became involved with Roger.

They re-renamed themselves Heart in 1975 and, with the support of Mushroom Records, released another "debut" album, *Dreamboat Annie*.

Signature songs: *Crazy On You, Barracuda, Magic Man*
Insight song: *City's Burning*

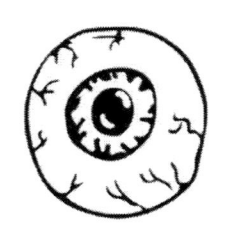

HEAVEN 17

These synth musicians formed their group in 1980 after quitting the band Human League. Both bands are from Sheffield, England, which was a real hotbed of new wave music in the eighties.

Heaven Seventeen is a fictional band mentioned in the Anthony Burgess novel, *A Clockwork Orange*. Furthermore, that fictional band hit number four on the charts with their fictional song "Inside."

Signature songs: *(We Don't Need) This Fascist Groove Thang, Temptation, Let Me Go*
Insight song: *This Is Mine*

HERE COME THE MUMMIES

This band's story is a gimmick, wrapped in another gimmick and stuffed deep inside a dirty secret.

They have declared that the entire band is actually thousands of years old and have been cursed by a great pharaoh for deflowering his daughter. Yes, the entire band. In addition to this elaborate origin story, the band members' identities are literally under wraps. They even play live shows disguised as mummies to hide their faces. The general rumor is that the band is comprised of Grammy winning musicians, who may or may not be under contract with other record companies. If you've heard them, this would come as no surprise.

But if it's a surprise you want, read no further because this band has a big one waiting for new listeners. Every song these mummies play is about one thing, sex. And not just sex, but intricately woven dirty scenarios, filthy imagery, puns galore, and all supported by some of the finest funk musicians of this or any age. In every category, they excel. Superb vocals, and all manner of instruments that can be strummed, banged, blown, or fingered. It's some of the most finely crafted filth on file. Now, go back and look at their band name again. See? It gets everywhere.

Signature songs: *Pants, Single Entendre*
Insight songs: *I Got You Covered, Everything But, You Know The Drill, Where The Sun Don't Shine*

THE HIVES

I think of The Hives as the Weezer of Sweden. Sweezer, if you will. This is meant as a compliment to both bands, as they both have the perfect amount of punk and pluck, plunk, if you will further.

Although the word hives is most commonly associated with bees, lead singer Per "Howlin' Pelle" Almqvist once said, "We're not a nest, we're definitely a rash. We get under people's skins."
Also, their hometown of Fagersta has a beautiful train station.

Signature songs: *Tick Tick Boom, Walk Idiot Walk, Hate To Say I Told You So.*
Insight song: *Good Samaritan*

HOLE

Here is another California punk band with a name designed to be shocking. In this case, Hole is meant to draw attention to the band's female energy in the form of lead singer and co-founder, Courtney Love's vagina. (See also, The Slits.) If that connection seems too far of a stretch, trust me, it's not. Their debut album is called *Pretty on the Inside*. However, if you prefer a more romantic view, it has been reported that Courtney's mother once told her that she "...can't go through life with a big hole in her, just because she had a bad childhood."

Signature songs: *Violet, Miss World, Doll Parts*
Insight songs: *Plump, Rock Star*

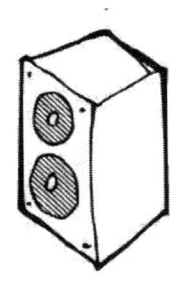

HOOBASTANK

The one you've all been waiting for. What the hell is Hoobastank? First of all, these guys are from Los Angeles. Agoura Hills to be more specific, but lead singer Doug Robb's brother worked in Germany. The siblings spoke often, but Doug had trouble pronouncing the name of the street his brother lived on, called Hoobustank. His version, Hoobastank, was something his brother occasionally teased him about.

When searching for a band name, many of their ideas were already taken. Hoobastank was suggested and, sure enough, no other band had chosen that name yet. It was completely original and even had a personal connection.

The band would also like to confirm that their name is not, as is often reported, named after a drunk person trying to pronounce scuba tank.

Signature song: *The Reason*
Insight song: *Born To Lead*

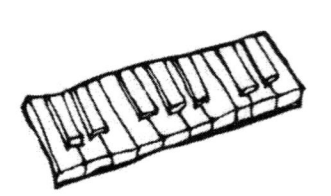

HOOTIE AND THE BLOWFISH

At first, it was just Darius Rucker and Mark Bryan playing mostly R.E.M. cover songs in and around Columbia, South Carolina. When Dean Felber joined the band, they did what all beginning bands did; they sat around and tried to come up with an attention getting name. According to myth, various nicknames in their

circle of friends included a kid with round glasses called Hootie, and a big cheeked horn player called Blowfish. They frequently top lists of worst band names ever, but for the record, I like that name, and them.
Signature songs: *Hold My Hand, Let Her Cry*
Insight songs: *Where Were You, Be The One*

THE HUMAN LEAGUE

Sheffield, England, 1977. Phillip Oakley founded his new electronic band with Martyn Ware and Ian Craig Marsh, who left the band after only one album to form Heaven 17. I find it fascinating that both bands begin with the letter *H*, and were inspired by a pop culture reference.

Human League began as The Future, but a more nuanced approach had them shuffle a few ideas around until they settled on something from the classic board game, Starforce Alpha Centauri. In the game, if a player makes it to the 25th century, they become aware of a group of people who seek more independence from planet Earth. They are known as the Human League.

Signature songs: *Human, Don't You Want Me, Mirror Man*
Insight song: *Together In Electric Dreams*

I

I DON'T KNOW HOW, BUT THEY FOUND ME
Known mostly as iDKHOW this pop duo formed in Salt Lake City, Utah, in 2016. Two years later, they were named by *Rock Sound* magazine as, "The hottest unsigned band in the world." Their name was taken from the 1985 film *Back to the Future* which makes me wonder why there aren't also bands named, Run For It! Marty! Or even better, If My Calculations Are Correct, When This Baby Hits Eighty-Eight Miles Per Hour, You're Gonna See Some Serious Shit. (IMCACWTBHEMPHYGSSSS for short).

Signature songs: *Do It All The Time, Choke, Leave Me Alone, Modern Day Cain*
Insight songs: *Clusterhug, Nobody Likes The Opening Band*

I'M FROM BARCELONA
Only a group from Sweden would pick a name like this. Like Canadians, the Swedish just have the most elegant sense of humor. The band consists of 28 members and has been active since 2005. Their sound is choral/classic/acoustic, like a pub full of singers who brought their own drums, practiced to get the

harmonies really tight, and then talked a few cousins into coming down to play guitar, or flute, or freakin' harp, whatever. This is all to say that they give off a vibe of comradery, and good times, but only if the non-drunk people sing.

They took their name from a character on the BBC television show *Faulty Towers* starring Monty Python's John Cleese. Manuel, played by Andrew Sachs, is from Barcelona and informs people thusly. The show only aired twelve episodes from 1975 to 1979.

Signature songs: *We're From Barcelona, Treehouse*
Insight song: *Paper Planes*

IMAGINE DRAGONS

One of the most recent and interesting band name mysteries lies with these Las Vegas musicians. The band's official statement is that the name is an anagram for another secret name, known only to the band members themselves. Lead singer Dan Reynolds is quoted as saying, "We really had a phrase that we all agreed upon, and had meaning to us, particularly as artists. We just thought it would be cool to keep something for ourselves because you're always exposing so much as an artist."

Fans have come up with thousands of guesses. Here is a (short) list of band names Imagine Dragons has officially denied as being the true anagram:

A Roaming Design
Radioman Egg Sin

Adorning Images
A Gemini So Grand
God Is In the Manger
Roman's Big Angie
Ragged Insomnia (Which appears on a bumper sticker in their video for "On Top of the World.")
They exploded on the scene with their debut album, *Night Visions*, and their power pop sound must have reminded everyone of how much they like Vertical Horizon and The Killers or something because all three bands got a boost in sales.
Signature songs: *Radioactive, Believer, Thunder*
Insight songs: *Underdog, Lonely*

INCUBUS
These indie/rock bandmates met in high school in Calabasas, California, and early on played famous venues like The Roxy and Whisky a Go Go. The name Incubus was picked from a book that did not explain what the word meant. When the band was told that an Incubus was a demon who violated sleeping women, they had already made their record deal. So, they kept it, hoping nobody would judge them too harshly. Also, metalheads seeing the name Incubus might be disappointed at their rather laid-back and occasionally romantic side.
Signature songs: *Drive, Pardon Me, Wish You Were Here*
Insight song: *Our Love*

INDIGO GIRLS

There is nothing wrong with picking a name just because it sounds good. After playing as The B Band, and Sailors & Ray, (as in Emily Sailors, and Amy Ray), the duo consulted a dictionary to give them some ideas for their modern folk rock. The word Indigo stuck out. Slap the word Girls behind it, and you got yourself a pretty decent band name. Fellow Athens rocker Michael Stipe lent the group some credence, providing guest vocals on their sophomore album, and containing the career making single "Closer To Fine".

Signature songs: *Closer To Fine, Shame On You*
Insight song: *Joking*

INFORMATION SOCIETY

This band formed in Dupre Hall at Macalester College in St. Paul. Their music, which often samples dialog from original *Star Trek* episodes, was considered avant-garde electronica when they owned the year 1988 with their monster single "What's On Your Mind (Pure Energy)".

Their name was inspired by a word in the fictional language of George Orwell's novel, *1984*. In *Newspeak*, the word *Ingsoc* is an abbreviation for English Socialism. Information Society, is known in the book as *InSoc*.

Signature songs: *Pure Energy (What's On Your Mind), Walking Away (Space Age Mix), Peace & Love Inc.*
Insight songs: *Come With Me, Mirrorshades, Can't Slow Down, Praying To The Aliens, Down In Flames*

INSANE CLOWN POSSE

This band was formed by two wrestlers who continued with WWE, and later the WCW, all while recording albums and getting a name for themselves musically. Originally the JJ Boys and Inner City, they decided to adopt a dark carnival theme as a way to distinguish themselves among other nineties rap and hip-hop acts. And thus, Insane Clown Posse was born. Their fans are affectionately known as Juggalos. The name has its roots in their song "The Juggla" and a famed 1994 concert performance.

Signature songs: *Jump Around, Hokus Pokus, Juggalo Island*
Insight song: *6 Foot 7 Foot (7 Foot 8 Foot Lyte)*

INXS

Pronounced, *In Excess*, you can see how clever the name must have felt for this emerging Sydney band in 1977. It wouldn't be until their fifth album, *Listen Like Thieves*, with their breakout single "What You Need" that INXS found their worldwide audience.

But that was only the beginning. *KICK*, their sixth studio album, launched the band into global stardom, and also has one of the all-time best music stories in a business filled with some real doozies. Band manager Chris Murphy took the newly recorded album to Atlantic records personally, and the brass hated it so much that they instructed him to offer the band one million dollars to scrap the whole thing and start again. Murphy told the band none of this and instead went to the promotions department and told them the orders from upstairs were to push the new single "Need You Tonight" on college radio.

The scheme worked and before anyone knew what happened, "Need You Tonight" was a radio smash and demand for a single went bonkers. *KICK* was soon scheduled to be released, but Atlantic was salty about the dupe and did little to promote the launch. Not that INXS needed the help. *KICK* was a top-ten album for over five months and spent a total of seventy-nine weeks on the *Billboard 200* chart.

Signature songs: *What You Need, New Sensation, Need You Tonight/Mediate, Suicide Blonde*
Insight songs: *Who Pays the Price, By My Side*

IRON & WINE

Sam Beam is from Chapin, South Carolina, but went to film school in Florida. He wound up as a professor of film and cinematography at the Miami International University of Art and Design. Music was just a hobby for him. He told *Spin Magazine* that when he was lighting a practical set for a film, shooting in an old gas station, he came across containers of home remedies. One of them was simply labeled, "Beef, Iron & Wine". He recalls knowing right away that if he dropped the beef, it would make a more interesting stage name than Sam Beam. As he tells it, it was finding the right name that flipped the switch. He liked the duality of something sweet and sour, something he liked to present in his music already.

He borrowed a four-track recorder from the brother of the lead singer of Band of Horses and began making demos. Through his equipment lending friend, Michael Bridewell, Sam's music came to the attention of *Yeti Magazine* and then Sub Pop Records. His song "Flightless Bird (American Mouth)" was famously championed by Kristen Stewart for the *Twilight* movie soundtrack.

Signature songs: *Such Great Heights, Flightless Bird (American Mouth)*

Insight songs: *Serpent Charmer, Carried Home, Arms Of A Thief, Peach Beneath The City*

IRON BUTTERFLY

This band was hoping to appeal to two sides of society in the mid-Sixties when they formed. There were people who liked hard rock, hence the name Iron. And there were those (hippies) who liked the softer side of music, hence the name Butterfly. They lived and played in San Diego until they hit it big, then they traveled the world where they were especially well-loved in Europe.

Signature song: *In A Gadda-Da-Vida*
Insight song: *In The Time Of Our Lives*

J

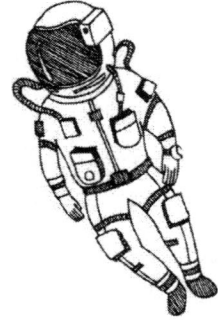

JAMIROQUAI

Jamiroquai is the combination of the words jam and Iroquai. The latter refers to the Iroquois Native Americans. It was the French who gave the powerful northeast natives the name Iroquois League. (Back then, Iroquois Confederacy.) They called themselves Haudenosaunee, which translates to "People of the Longhouse".

This might all seem odd since band founder Jason Kay is from London, but he had a rough start in life. Music gave him the outlet, focus, and purpose he needed to turn himself around. The musical persona was a part of that.

Jamiroquai has an eclectic sound, mixing elements seemingly at random, not unlike Beck. His songwriting is constantly strong. He won just about every award there was to win with his breakout single "Virtual Insanity." Furthermore, the 1996 album it came from, *Traveling Without Moving*, earned the Guinness World Record of best-selling funk album in history.

Signature songs: *Virtual Insanity, Canned Heat*
Insight songs: *Cosmic Girl, Space Cowboy*

JANE'S ADDICTION

From Los Angeles, and birthed from the ashes of Perry Farrell's former band, Psi-Com, the Jane in Jane's Addiction is a real person. Her drug addiction was also very real. The two were roommates and she inspired not only the band's name but a new song "Jane Says" which became their first hit.

Farrell's girlfriend at the time, Casey Niccoli, suggested Jane's Heroin Experience for the band name when they were in the car one day. Farrell was intrigued but not sold. He felt that if you wanted to welcome people in, you don't put heroin on your door. They settled on something less specific and wound up with Jane's Addiction.

Their music is a mixture of metal, funk and, at times, a little psychedelic. The arresting vocals by Farrell are matched by guitarist Dave Navarro's infamously wicked shredding.

Signature songs: *Been Caught Stealing, Stop!, Jane Says*
Insight songs: *My Cat's Name Is Maceo, Pigs In Zen, Irresistible Force, The Riches, Idiots Rule*

JAPANDROIDS

A guitar, a few drums, and two mics. That's all these two British Columbian musicians need to make a lot of noise. They play good old-fashioned rock and roll.

The band name came from a brainstorming session where David Prowse (not the actor in the Darth Vader suit) suggested Japanese Scream. Brian King suggested Pleasure Droids. The latter was likely taken from Stephen Spielberg's underrated film *A.I.* where the term first appeared in pop culture. They combined the names to create Japandroids.

Signature songs: *The House That Heaven Built, Younger Us*
Insight song: *The Boys Are Leaving Town*

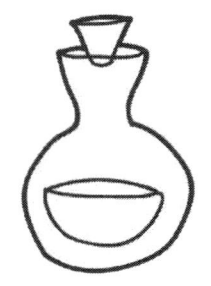

JARS OF CLAY
2 Corinthians 4:7 "But we have this treasure in jars of clay to show that all surpassing power is from God and not from us." A fitting band name for these Christian rockers. This verse is actually summed up on a hidden track at the end of their 1995 self-titled debut album. The band is based in Nashville, Tennessee, but the members met at Greenville College in Illinois.

Signature song: *Flood*
Insight song: *Liquid*

JEFFERSON AIRPLANE / JEFFERSON STARSHIP / STARSHIP / and, for some reason, HOT TUNA?
This band was a big part of the acid rock scene in San Francisco. They sometimes leaned more toward folk rock but, like Grateful Dead, sometimes went full-on psychedelic.

They amended their name every time they had a line-up shuffle. Except for their very first substitution when Grace Slick took over lead vocals for Signe Toly Anderson. They also had at least one hit song with each iteration of the band.

The first name started as a joke, poking fun at old blues monikers. A friend suggested Blind Lemon Jefferson Airplane, and the band liked half of it. The later incarnations have an easy to follow progression; they were just trying to get closer and closer to the stars.

Hot Tuna was formed when Starship split for good. They wanted to call themselves Hot Shit, thinking it would be funny to take over the musical scene with such a name. Their record company talked them out of it.

As Jefferson Airplane:
Signature songs: *White Rabbit, Somebody To Love*
Insight song: *Volunteers*

As Jefferson Starship:
Signature song: *Jane*
Insight song: *Stranger*

As Starship:
Signature songs: *We Built This City, Nothing's Gonna Stop Us Now, Sara*
Insight song: *It's Not Enough*

As Hot Tuna:
Signature song: *Keep On Truckin'*
Insight song: *Death Don't Have No Mercy*

JET

This Millburn, Australia, band was founded by brothers, Nic and Chris Chester. Their father's classic rock record collection, along with Australian band You Am I, inspired them to pick up instruments and play. Their style is raw, blues rock. A throwback vibe for a band that formed in 2001. They could open for the Stones.

They wanted to pick a band name that was powerful but short, so it would be bigger on festival posters. Ingenious!

Signature songs: *Are You Gonna Be My Girl?, Cold Hard Bitch*
Insight songs: *Get What You Need, Lazy Gun*

JOHNNY HATES JAZZ

This London based duo were already working together when they visited the sister of Mike Nocito. He and his bandmate, Clark Datchler, observed that while Lisa loved jazz music, and frequently played it in the house, her husband, John, disliked it intensely, and vocally. They coined the phrase Johnny Hates Jazz and planned to do something with it. That something wound up being their band name.

Signature songs: *Shattered Dreams, I Don't Want To Be A Hero,*
Insight songs: *Magnetized, Heart Of Gold*

JOY DIVISION

This is another case of a famous band that became another famous band. These blokes are from Salford, England, and started off by calling themselves Warsaw, which was a reference to the David Bowie song, "Warszawa." But it's the same old story, another band was already using the name. In this case, a local band called Warsaw Pakt.

They came up with the much sunnier sounding Joy Division, but while the name is pleasant it has dark roots. *The Joy Division* was the name of the sexual slavery wing in a Nazi concentration camp described in the 1955 novel *House of Dolls* written by holocaust survivor Yehiel De-Nur aka Ka-Tsetnik 135633.

This was in 1978. By 1980 the band would be darlings of the UK and about to embark on their first USA/Canada tour. On May 18th, 1980, lead singer Ian Curtis hung himself. He had attempted suicide the year before with an overdose, but all concerned thought he had worked through his issues. An impending divorce is believed to have been a contributing factor.

The surviving duo gained some more members and became New Order. Another Nazi reference, by the way, but we'll get into that in the "N" section.

Signature songs: *Love Will Tear Us Apart, Disorder*
Insight song: *Heart And Soul*

JUDAS PRIEST

Birmingham, England. The home of *British Steel*. This is the name of the 1980 album that would finally put Judas Priest on the global map. It was their sixth studio effort, which means that people who already knew them in the seventies were the lucky ones.

Considered one of the pioneers of heavy metal, they actually took their name from a Bob Dylan song. "The Ballad of Frankie Lee and Judas Priest" can be heard on the late 1967 release, *John Wesley Harding*.

Signature songs: *Breaking the Law, You've Got Another Thing Coming, Painkiller*

Insight song: *Heading Out To The Highway*

JURASSIC 5

L.A. rappers in the early nineties were trying to push the game forward, but these five musicians were cool with old school. Founding member Chali 2na gave his son a copy of their first recorded song, "Unified Rebelution," and he then played it for his mother. She grooved with their classic sound and later told Chali, "You guys think you're the Fantastic 5." This was a reference to legendary rap artist Grandwizard Theodore & the Fantastic Five. Chali recalls getting the idea for a band name in that moment and joked, "We sound more like the Jurassic 5."

Signature songs: *What's Golden, Quality Control*
Insight song: *Ducky Boy*

K

KAJAGOOGOO

Bassist Nick Beggs begs everyone not to take their group's name too seriously. It's quite literally baby speak. This new wave Bedfordshire, England, band exploded on the scene in 1983 with their massive hit "Too Shy" but they actually started five years before as the band, Art Noveau.

Unhappy with their lead singer, they hired a new one and chose a new name taken from a phrase that many infants use, ga ga goo goo. They altered it a bit, and Kajagoogoo was the result. Something forgettable and unforgettable at the same time.

Signature songs: *Too Shy, Hang On Now*
Insight song: *Big Apple*

KASABIAN

If you've heard the name before perhaps it was because of Linda Kasabian, a well-known member of the Charles Manson "Family," who testified against Manson in exchange for immunity. The name was pitched to the group by former guitar player Chris Karloff, who noted that the name kept jumping off the page as he read about the Manson case. According to bass player Chris Edwards the band sat with the name for about a minute before they knew it was

right for them. They hail from the heart of England, in Leicester, and carry on a long tradition of dynamic music making in Fog Town.
Signature songs: *Club Foot, Bumblebee*
Insight songs: *Doomsday, Stevie, El Ray, Let's Roll Just Like We Used To*

KEANE

Lead singer Tom Chaplin has explained that as a boy he was fond of his mother's friend, Cherry Keane. Her name always reminded him of the term, Peachy Keen. He called his band by her whole name at first, but soon dropped the Cherry. They became simply, Keane.
Signature songs: *Somewhere Only We Know, Is It Any Wonder*
Insight song: *Tear Up This Town*

KENTUCKY HEADHUNTERS

While it's not uncommon for a band to have had other monikers before settling on a final creative choice, these guys operated under a different name for almost fifteen years! From 1968 to 1982, they were Itchy Brother. (Named so for the Young brothers on rhythm guitar and drums.)
After a four-year hiatus from their country rocking, they re-banded and re-branded as The Headhunters. This was a nod to Muddy Waters' legendary band, The Head

Choppers. (The Head Choppers were named as a braggadocio way of saying they would musically decapitate all other bands in their way.)

When The Headhunters discovered that the name was already in use, they added their home state to the name.

Signature song: *Walk Softly On This Heart Of Mine*
Insight song: *My Daddy Was A Milkman*

THE KILLERS

These Las Vegas musicians were big fans of New Order, and took their name from a video for the 2001 song "Crystal." In the video, New Order is playing on stage as a band called The Killers.

Their music is emotional and inventive, without being exhausting or confusing. They hit the sweet spot, in other words.

Signature songs: *Somebody Told Me, Mr. Brightside*
Insight song: *Wonderful Wonderful*

THE KINGSMEN

Why is "Louie Louie" the Washington state rock song? I couldn't tell you, because The Kingsmen are from Portland. Most of the members had played together since junior high school, but became official in 1959 when they took the name from another band that had broken up.

They recorded "Louie Louie" in 1963. It was standard practice at that time for budding bands to cover that song.

In fact, only a few days later, Paul Revere and the Raiders recorded their version in the exact same Portland studio.

Both songs fought it out on radio stations in the Pacific Northwest for months before a Boston DJ got a hold of the Kingsmen version. The East Coast ate it up, and the band signed with a New York label called Wand.

Their first full length LP was a live recording from Milwaukie, Oregon.

Signature song: *Louie Louie*
Insight song: *Death Of An Angel*

KINGS OF LEON

This Nashville based band keeps it all in the family. Made up of three brothers and their cousin, they decided to pay tribute to the patriarch of the family with their band name. Southern preacher Ivan Leon Followill used to drive his three boys around in a purple Oldsmobile where they would often bang on drums during tent revival services.

Their blues rock style never forgets their country roots, but doesn't dig too deep there either. They sound straight alternative for whole albums at a time.

Signature songs: *Sex On Fire, Use Somebody*
Insight songs: *Rock City, Trunk, Pony Up*

KING CRIMSON

Although these progressive rockers had been playing together for over a year, they officially became King Crimson on January 13, 1969. They took their name from one of their own songs called "The Court Of The Crimson King." They are yet another London band who continue to have a huge influence on music lovers. Now you can see why I want to follow-up this book with one exploring each city's musical timeline and overall influence on band culture.

Signature songs: *Moonchild, The Court Of The Crimson King, Epitaph*
Insight song: *21st Century Schizoid Man*

KISS

All band members deny that the name was ever an acronym for "Knights In Satan's Service." Paul Stanley has stated that the name KISS was chosen because it sounded both sexy and dangerous. This notion has since been corroborated by various other band members.

Signature song: *Rock & Roll All Nite*
Insight song: *Beth*

KRAFTWERK

German musicians have always been extra experimental, and this group is widely considered as the grandfathers of electronic music. Kraftwerk is the

German word for power station. They wanted a name that came from everyday life because they used every day sounds as the bedrock of their music. (Kraftwerk's early seventies electro-music was dubbed as Krautrock, which seems super racist to me, but I've been assured that it's cool.)

Power Station as a name was also good enough to have an English counterpart, the short-lived supergroup once fronted by Robert Palmer.

Signature song: *Pocket Calculator*
Insight song: *The Robots*

KONGOS

Kongos is the last name of the band's entire line-up. All brothers, just like Hansen. Ordinarily I wouldn't include either in this collection, and in the case of Hansen, I didn't. However, Kongos name origin was not so obvious, and if Kings Of Leon gets a paragraph then so should Kongos. (I'm still not going back to do one for Hansen though.)

The band is from South Africa, but is now based in Phoenix. You will not hear better accordion playing in your life, not even by a certain Mr. "Weird Al" Yankovic. (To whom I bow.)

Signature song: *Come With Me Now*
Insight song: *I Don't Mind*

KORN

For the record, this L.A. band knows they have a dumb name, so that's something. James Shaffer, rhythm guitarist and band founder, suggested the name Corn but it was immediately rejected by the rest of the guys. He later suggested it with a logo he designed that showed the name spelled with a *K*, and a backward capital *R*. It was accepted with the understanding that once they were established, the name wouldn't matter.

Signature song: *Freak On A Leash*
Insight song: *Got The Life*

L

L.A. GUNS

Tracii Guns was from L.A. and started a rock band. Boom! Most succinct opening sentence in this book!

This is the group that merged with Hollywood Rose, fronted by Axl Rose. (See also, Guns N' Roses.) Tracii was eventually booted, and the band became Guns N' Roses.

He reclaimed his band, L.A. Guns, and continues to record. Thirteen studio albums and counting.

Signature song: *The Ballad Of Jayne*
Insight song: *Let You Down*

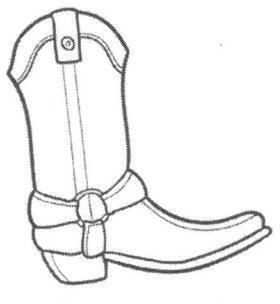

THE LAZY COWGIRLS

Pat Todd, who wrote the Foreword for this book, told me that his band was making good music in the L.A. area, and ready to choose a name. So, he instructed band members to bring fifty suggestions to the next rehearsal. Before that day, Pat heard Neil Young's "Cowgirl in the Sand" on the radio. The word *cowgirl* resonated with him and, with multiple band members, the group would have to be the cowgirls. "But what kind of cowgirls?" was the question. The band went through the formality of considering hundreds of other names at the next rehearsal but The Lazy Cowgirls was already a frontrunner for Pat, who liked that it played down the macho rock music scene and helped everybody, including the band, not to take themselves too seriously.

Signature songs: *Goddamn Bottle, The Long Goodbye*
Insight songs: *Justine, Still On The Losin' Side, Cold Cold World, Justine (Cover)*

LED ZEPPELIN

This band was going to be huge even before it had a name. By 1966, Jimmy Page was leading the Yardbirds, which he renamed The New Yardbirds, and kicking around the idea of a starting a new band while recording "Beck's Borelo" with Keith Moon, John Entwistle, Jeff Beck, and John Paul Jones.

According to myth, Keith Moon said the project would go over like a lead balloon, but Entwistle insisted that it was he who made the joke.

Either way, Page remembered the comment two years later when he formed and named the London based supergroup, Led Zeppelin. They recorded their first four albums in two years while on constant tour.

Signature songs: *Whole Lotta Love, Black Dog, Stairway To Heaven, Kashmir*
Insight song: *In The Light*

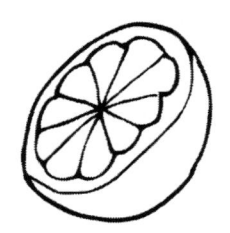

LEMONHEADS

Did this band actually name themselves after the candy of the same name? Yes. Yes, they did. Originally known as Whelps, these Boston boys had played together since they were teenagers. Front man Evan Dando has described the band as much like the candy, "Sweet on the inside, and sour on the outside."

The indie rock scene was not welcoming at first, but the band's fifth studio album, *It's a Shame About Ray,* helped them break through to the mainstream, as did a cover of "Mrs. Robinson," which is heard in the film *Wayne's World 2*, and also more recently in *The Wolf of Wall Street.*

Signature song: *It's A Shame About Ray*

Insight songs: *If I Could Talk I'd Tell You, My Drug Buddy*

LINKIN PARK

The late Chester Bennington used to drive past Lincoln Park in Santa Monica, California, on his way to record with his newly formed band. They fiddled with the park's spelling to obtain a web domain. Their first album was a massive success and their combination of hard rock and rap elements, courtesy of Mike Shinoda, set them apart from other heavy acts in the nineties.

Signature songs: *Numb, Leave Out All The Rest, Breaking The Habit*

Insight songs: *When They Come For Me, Iridescent*

LIPPS INC.

This band was started by wedding DJ Steven Greenberg in Minneapolis, Minnesota. He was a solo act until he auditioned Cynthia Johnson for a song he wrote called "Rock It." This disco duo was born and got noticed with the song, but really hit the big time with their next single "Funkytown." The song hit No. 1 on the Billboard charts in over a dozen countries by May 1980, and stayed there for a month. It pretty much owned that summer too, and the summer after that.

The original idea was to name the band Lip Sync, but that name was taken. So, they spelled it Lipps Inc. instead.

Signature song: *Funkytown*
Insight song: *Power*

LITTLE RIVER BAND

This band is named after the Little River in Melbourne's state of Victoria. Most people think they're from Nashville, but they're actually the first Australian band to enjoy consistent commercial success in America. Only INXS would eventually make it bigger, but that wouldn't be until ten years after this Melbourne band formed. (Actually, both bands formed at roughly the same time, but it took INXS longer to get a global stage.)

Harmony rock was all the rage in the seventies, and these guys did that as good as Kansas. It's probably why

everybody assumed they were another southern rock band from the States. Their name didn't help. Or did it?
Signature songs: *Lonesome Loser, Help Is On The Way, Happy Anniversary*
Insight song: *The Night Owls*

LIVE
Once known as Public Affection, this group developed a reputation as a great band to see live when in York, Pennsylvania. I wish I had more than that. I can tell you that they are the only band in history with a hit single that includes the word placenta. So, that's a feather in their caps. Their sophomore album, *Throwing Copper,* produced five singles and hit No. 1 on the Billboard 200 chart exactly one year after it was released.
Signature songs: *Lightning Crashes, Pain Lies On the Riverside, The Beauty Of Gray*
Insight songs: *Good Pain, The Dam At Otter Creek*

LOVE AND ROCKETS
This Brit band was made up of three members of Bauhaus after the group split up in 1983. They took their name from an alternative comic book series. They rode the new wave from Europe to America.
Signature song: *So Alive*
Insight song: *No Big Deal*

LOVIN' SPOONFUL

Folk music exploded in Greenwich Village in the fifties and sixties and influenced these childhood bandmates, who also play rock and jazz. They took their name from the lyrics in "Coffee Blues" by "Mississippi" John Hurt.

Front man John Sebastian's little brother, Mark, was just fifteen when he wrote a poem the band would use as the basis of the song "Summer in the City." John has spoken about how he particularly liked the line, "But at night there's a different world." Mark later recounted that he was just happy they kept his opening rhyme.

John Lennon revealed that "Good Day Sunshine" was more than a passing nod to Lovin' Spoonful's "Daydream."

Signature songs: *Summer In The City, Do You Believe In Magic, Daydream*
Insight song: *Rain On The Roof*

LYNYRD SKYNYRD

Probably the best known southern rock band in history, and half of the population still thinks the group was a single guy named Leonard.

The truth isn't as far off as one might think. Founding members, Bob Burns and Gary Rossington, named the band after their real life gym teacher, Leonard Skinner, who often harassed the duo for their long hair while they

attended Robert E. Lee High in Jacksonville, Florida. For a while they called themselves One Percent, and then Nobel Five, but Lynyrd Skynyrd just rolls off the tongue, and the nod to their biggest critic is bold and hilarious.
Signature songs: *Freebird, Sweet Home Alabama*
Insight song: *Saturday Night Special*

M

MAE
Mae stands for morning, afternoon, and evening. They're from one of my favorite cities, Norfolk, Virginia, which also boasts the biggest Naval base in the USA. Another highly underrated band, they play alternative rock with a ton of piano and, although not a Christian band strictly speaking, their spirituality shines through.
Signature song: *Embers And Envelopes*
Insight songs: *Anything from their 2005 album, The Everglow.*

MANHATTAN TRANSFER
Even though this vocal quartet is from New York City, *Manhattan Transfer* is the name of the 1925 novel by John Dos Passos. Since 1969, the band has undergone dozens of line-up changes and released twenty-nine albums.
Signature songs: *Boy From New York City, Java Jive, Birdland, Trickle Trickle*
Insight songs: *Coo Coo U, The Speak Up Mambo* (Cover)

MARCY PLAYGROUND
Marcy Playground is the name of the playground at Marcy Open Grade School in Minneapolis. This power

trio is based in New York City now, but many songs are still inspired by front man John Wozniak's childhood in Minnesota.

Signature song: *Sex & Candy*
Insight song: *The Devil's Song*

MARILLION

From Aylesbury, England, Marillion straddled the punk and progressive rock genres. Their name is an alteration on the title of the 1977 J. R. R. Tolkein (posthumous) novel *The Silmarillion*.

Signature songs: *Kayleigh, Alice*
Insight songs: *Fugazi, Freaks*

MAROON 5

From 1994 to 2001, this band called themselves Karla's Flowers but made a change just before they hit it big with their debut album, *Songs About Jane*. Like Imagine Dragons or Pearl Jam, whose name is the subject of much speculation and rumor, Adam Levine once told David Letterman, "The origin of the name is so bad. It's such a horrendous story that we decided that shrouding it in mystery will make a better story than the actual story."

Some fans have reasoned that since some of the band members went to Five Towns College in Long Island, as well as having five members in the group, that part of the name is no real stretch of the imagination. However, the college mascot is the Sounds, a nifty musical nod when you consider that the school colors are maroon and white. (My guess is that the name White 5 was quickly dismissed in favor of Maroon 5.)

Not only does this story seem reasonable, it's just boring enough for the bandmates to assign it more negative baggage than it deserves. I think it's a great throwback name to the vocal bands of the fifties.

Signature songs: *She Will Be Loved, Misery, One More Night, This Love, Maps, Moves Like Jagger, Memories*
Insight song: *Not Coming Home, Remedy*

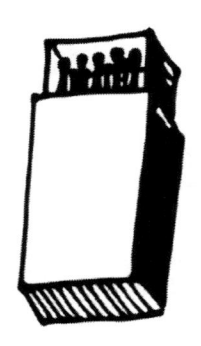

MATCHBOX TWENTY

These fellas are from Orlando, and took their name from a softball jersey. The jersey had a big number 20 and a patch that read Matchbox. In fact, when they took the world by storm in 1996 with their debut album, *Yourself, Or Someone Like You*, they used the number 20 instead of spelling it out like they do now.

Signature songs: *3AM, Real World*
Insight song: *She's So Mean*

MEN WITHOUT HATS

This band started out on Montreal stages as Men With Hats, which they then threw into the audience at the end of the show. They thought it would be cheaper in the long run to change their name to Men *Without* Hats. Once again, proving how funny Canadians are.

Signature songs: *Safety Dance, Pop Goes The World*
Insight songs: *Ideas For Walls, The Great Ones*

METALLICA

The story goes that band drummer Lars Ulrich was once helping a friend come up with names for a magazine for metal music fans. The magazine was eventually called *Metal Mania*, but Lars remembered another one of the suggestions, Metallica, and used it for his own Los Angeles based metal band.

Signature songs: *For Whom The Bell Tolls, Nothing Else Matters, Enter Sandman, Master of Puppets*
Insight song: *Now That We're Dead*

RUSS MEYER SUBSECTION:
This film director has four bands named after his movies!

1. FASTER PUSSYCAT
L.A. heavy metal band with better hair than Lita Ford and Dee Snider put together! Their name was taken from the 1965 film, *Faster Pussycat! Kill! Kill!*
Signature songs: *House Of Pain, Poison Ivy*
Insight song: *Where There's A Whip There's A Way*

2. MOTORPSYCHO
These Prog rock Norwegians (not a bad band name right there), took their name from the 1965 film of the same name.
Signature song: *Have Fun*
Insight song: *Mad Sun*

3. MUDHONEY
Grunge rockers from Seattle that coalesced after the demise of Green River. Their name was taken from the 1965 film of the same name.
Signature songs: *Touch Me I'm Sick, Suck You Dry*
Insight song: *Kill Yourself Live*

4. VIXEN
Lady rockers from St. Paul, who took their name from the title of Meyer's 1968 film offering.
Signature song: *Edge Of A Broken Heart*
Insight song: *I Try*

MIAMI SOUND MACHINE

When Emilio Estefan heard Gloria sing at a wedding, he asked her to join his band The Miami Latin Boys. They had to change their name, of course, and became Miami Sound Machine. Meanwhile, Emilio and Gloria fell in love and got married. Their album, *Primitive Love*, owned 1985 (along with a-ha's *Hunting High and Low*.) The fascinating thing is, *Primitive Love* was Miami Sound Machine's ninth studio release! They mixed pop and Latin sounds with Gloria's strong voice, and just kept running that play until the rest of the world started clapping.

Signature songs: *Bad Boy, Conga*
Insight songs: *Dr. Beat, Orange Express*

MISFITS

This band definitely has that L.A. punk vibe, but it was founded in Lodi, New Jersey, by Glenn Danzig. Even for a punk band, these guys were intense. The term "Horror Punk" was invented just to describe their sound. The interesting thing is, even though Glenn can scream with the best of 'em, he's also a crooner who sounds at times like Jim Morrison. And on their song "American Nightmare" he sounds like Buddy Holly doing an Elvis impression!

Glenn left the band in 1983 to form Samhain but unreleased Misfits music kept getting pressed, including the entirety of their debut album, *Static Age*, which was shelved until 1996. They took their name from the 1961 film of the same name.

Signature songs: *Die Die My Darling, Mommy Can I Go Out and Kill Tonight?, Who Killed Marylin?*

Insight songs: *Where Eagles Dare, Bullet, I Turned Into A Martian, Theme For A Jackal, She, Return Of The Fly, TV Casualty, Attitude*

MODEST MOUSE

With a name taken from the 1917 Virginia Woolf (stream of consciousness) book about the inner workings of the human mind, this is the thinking man's band. The book is called *The Mark on the Wall*, and their debut album, *This is a Long Drive for Someone With Nothing to Think About,* is equally provocative.

Modest Mouse formed in Issaquah, Washington, but are now based in Portland - a good town for a punky/progressive band like them. Other album titles I like in their discography include, *Good News for People Who Love Bad News*, and *We Were Dead Before the Ship Even Sank*.

Signature songs: *Ice Cream Party, Float On*
Insight song: *Lampshades On Fire*

MOGWAI

These space rockers are from Glasgow. Their name was taken from the 1984 film, *Gremlins*. Mogwai is the Chinese word for the little creatures. The band makes such good instrumental music that they have been recruited to do many soundtracks for movies and video games alike. Most notably would be the score for the emotionally charged teen choice based game *Life Is Strange*.

Signature songs: *Richie Sacramento, Dry fantasy*
Insight song: *Take Me Somewhere Nice*

MOLOKO

This English/Irish duo got their name from a movie and, even though I've already listed a hundred and one other bands that have gotten their name from pop culture, Moloko is a personal favorite reference. They got their name from a particularly funny part of a particularly dark movie.

Moloko is the Russian word for milk, and it's what Alex and the Droogs drink in Stanley Kubrick's cult film *A Clockwork Orange*. Moloko in the movie is not as innocent as it seems. The same could be said for the band. Moloko is impossible to define and should not be dismissed as a novelty band. These two are up to something the rest of us will need to catch up to.

Signature songs: *Sing It Back, Pure Pleasure Seeker*
Insight song: *Party Weirdo*

THE MOODY BLUES

The band was once known as The M&B 5, named for the Mitchells & Butlers brewery in Birmingham, England. They later changed to The Moody Blues, inspired by the Duke Ellington song "Mood Indigo."
Blues music does play a part in the band's overall sound but a progressive streak, as well as a cornucopia of trippy imagery, keep their audience guessing.
Signature song: *Nights In White Satin*
Insight song: *Forever Autumn*

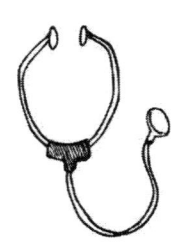

MÖTLEY CRÜE

Los Angeles eighties glam rock at its finest. Word is that guitarist Mick Mars was telling his bandmates about a comment made by a member of his former band, White Horse. The observation was that Mick's new band was "A motley looking crew." The band chose that as their name right there and then, but spelled it with umlauts like the German beer, Löwenbräu, they were drinking.
Signature songs: *Dr. Feelgood, Wildside, Smokin' In The Boys Room*
Insight song: *The Dirt*

MUSE

Although Matthew Bellamy, the band's lead singer, claims the name just looked striking on promotional posters, there is more to the story. Their hometown of Teignmouth, England, produces an inordinate number of artists, actors, and musicians. It's been long believed that a muse hangs over the city. This is where the bandmates first came across the word.

Signature song: *Uprising*
Insight song: *Knights Of Cydonia*

MUTEMATH

This band began as an electric duo in New Orleans, Louisiana, with Darren King, one of rock 'n' roll's all-time great drummers, and Paul Meany, keyboardist, vocalist, and future producer of the Twenty-One Pilots album, *Trench*. They called themselves Math, at first. It looked good and felt good on the tongue, but another band had already registered that name. Mutemath was their solution. It still looked good. It still sounded good, and it looked even better on paper, so that's what they went with.

Signature song: *Spotlight*
Insight songs: *You Are Mine, War, Armistice, Goodbye, Break The Fever*

MY BLOODY VALENTINE

With a band name taken from the 1981 horror movie of the same name, these rockers aren't as glum sounding as one might suspect. They're quite dreamy, in fact. Maybe that's because they're from Dublin, and Irish people are too sarcastic to be depressed.

Signature songs: *Sometimes, Swallow, Soon*
Insight song: *To Here Knows When*

MY CHEMICAL ROMANCE

Lead singer Gerard Way was going to have a nervous breakdown in Japan, but instead he wrote a concept album about getting cancer called *The Black Parade*. It was the band's third studio album and propelled them into super stardom. Since they're from Newark, New Jersey, they're already located near the cheapest airport into or out of New York City, which was helpful on tour.

Their heavy, yet emotional, style of music makes them accessible to people who are juggling many feelings all at once. The band name is an alteration on the title of the 1996 Irvine Welsh short story collection, *Ecstasy, Three Takes of Chemical Romance*.

Signature songs: *Helena, Welcome To The Black Parade*
Insight songs: *Mama, Blood, Famous Last Words*

N

NERF HERDER

As in, "scruffy-looking Nerf Herder," which is what Princess Leia calls Han Solo in the 1980 *Star Wars* sequel, *The Empire Strikes Back*.

This Santa Barbara, California, band has a musical style that fits their name. Subtle but funny, and a little edgy too. Not as loose musically as The Dead Milkmen, but not as controlled as The Offspring either. It's a good mix.

Signature song: *Van Halen*
Insight songs: *Nosering Girl, Ghostbusters III*

THE NETWORK

This was a secret side project by the band Green Day along with some friends. Their only album *Money Money 2020*, actually released back in 2003, is fantastic and funny. Since the whole thing was a gag, then a footnote, I don't know how they picked the name. But I had to include them anyway because this "N" section is pretty lean.

Signature song: *Money Money 2020*
Insight song: *Spike*

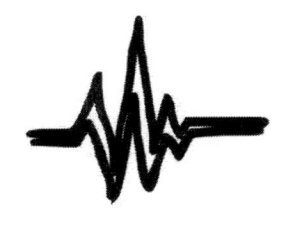

NEW ORDER

Built from the tragedy of Joy Division's break up due to the lead singer's suicide. Bernard Sumner took over the duties of lead singer, and the group recruited Stephen Morris's girlfriend, Gillian Gilbert, for keyboard and guitar.

New Order joined the likes of Erasure, Depeche Mode, and Duran Duran as one of the most successful Europop acts of the eighties.

Did they know they would be called Nazis for using this name? Yes. Yes, they did. But it was never meant to offend. Although they tried other names on for size, they simply preferred New Order.

The group was so popular, and had so many hit singles, that they successfully changed the meaning of the term for younger generations. Today, the band is the first thing Google brings up when you search New Order.

Signature songs: *Blue Monday, The Perfect Kiss*
Insight song: *Bizarre Love Triangle*

NEW RIDERS OF THE PURPLE SAGE

The origin of this band is centered on Jerry Garcia, who used to play country/beatnik gigs at the Perry Lane housing complex. This was on the Stanford University campus in Menlo Park, California. He would also form The Warlocks at this time, the earliest version of what would become Grateful Dead.

The band name is a variation on the title of the 1912 Zane Grey novel, *Riders of the Purple Sage.*
Signature songs: *Glendale Train, I Don't Know You*
Insight songs: *Portland Woman, Lonesome L.A. Cowboy*

NEW YORK DOLLS

Billy Murcia and Sylvain Sylvain both worked at a NYC clothes shop called *Truth and Soul.* The business was located across the street from the famed New York Doll Hospital, which was the subject of many conversations. When Sylvain suggested that New York Dolls would be a good name for a band, they formed a band so they could *be* that band.
Signature song: *Personality Crisis*
Insight song: *Subway Train*

NIGHT RANGER

You know it's a good band when its lineage can be traced back to Sly and the Family Stone. Jerry Martini formed the one-hit wonder band Rubicon which then became Stereo, then Ranger. Ranger sounded mysterious, dangerous even. They played all over San Francisco as Ranger and even opened for Sammy Hagar.
When a country band called The Rangers claimed copyright infringement, they changed their name to Night Ranger. They liked that better anyway, it sounded more mysterious, more dangerous even.
Signature song: *Sister Christian*
Insight song: *The Secret Of My Success*

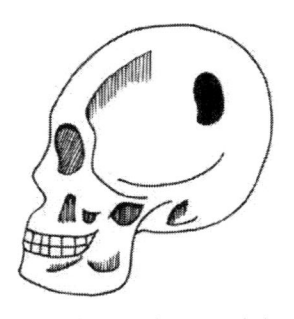

NINE INCH NAILS

This Cleveland solo act did something solo acts rarely do. He added another band member. Trent Reznor earned Academy Awards for the film scores of *The Social Network* and *Soul* in collaboration with musician and producer, Atticus Ross. The two men have worked professionally together since 2005, but just before Nine Inch Nails released the first in their *Bad Witch* trilogy in 2016, Ross was officially listed as a member of the band. The fellow songwriters continue to work as NIN as well as scoring films under their normal human names.

Trent Reznor chose Nine Inch Nails because it sounded "hard" and abbreviated nicely to NIN. (Sorry, I can't turn that last N backward.) He considered hundreds of ideas, and they all felt stupid after a single night. When Nine Inch Nails passed the two-week mark, and it still didn't feel dumb, he stuck with it.

Signature songs: *Head Like A Hole, Closer, Hurt, The Hand That Feeds*
Insight songs: *The Only Time, Getting Smaller*

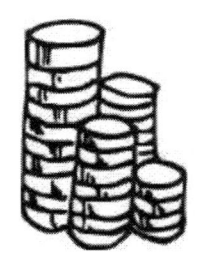

NICKELBACK

These Canadians started as a cover band called Village Idiot. They coalesced their sound and changed their name to a phrase that bassist Mike Kroeger said a lot while

working at Starbucks, "Here's your nickel back."
Signature songs: *Photograph, How You Remind Me*
Insight song: *Animals*

NIRVANA

This famed Seattle power trio started out considering silly names for their band. Names like Pen Cap Chew and Ted Ed Fred were rejected for something Kurt Cobain eventually suggested. He tested out a beautiful sounding name, something that would offset their sound. Something like, Nirvana.

Their sophomore album, *Nevermind*, had a huge impact on music. Although Nirvana is credited with the birth of grunge, it was not a widely used word at the time. *Nevermind* was considered Seattle's version of punk.

Each city has its own sound. You can often tell an L.A. band from a New York band. Seattle bands languished in their songs and had been serving up minor chord mope-rock for a while by the time Nirvana's harsh vibe woke up the whole industry. They led the way for groups like Pearl Jam, Soundgarden, and Smashing Pumpkins, feeding a new hunger for music that was deliberate in sound. Hundreds of punk/grunge/thrash/alternative bands have achieved fame due to *Nevermind*'s popularity.

Signature songs: *Smells Like Teen Spirit, Come As You Are, Heart Shaped Box, Something's In The Way*
Insight song: *Negative Creep*

NO DOUBT

From Anaheim, California, the land of Disney, this band got its name long before it got its famous lead singer, Gwen Stefani. It was the band's original singer, John Spence, who named the band after his favorite expression whenever he agreed with someone. "No doubt."

Signature songs: *Don't Speak, Just A Girl*
Insight song: *Ex-Girlfriend*

NOFX

Bands from Los Angeles always seem to put a lot of thought into their names. This handle is a rejection of gimmickry, as in no effects. It is also a nod to the band that influenced their music, Negative FX.

Signature song: *Separation Of Church And Skate*
Insight song: *The Decline*

THE NUMBER TWELVE LOOKS LIKE YOU

Mathcore is hardcore metal music but with irregular time signatures, and complicated sequences. You know, the kinds of things a bunch of New Jersey nerds would do if all the tubas and trombones suddenly disappeared. (Just kidding all you horny bastards!)

Even though having a number in their band name is the

perfect touch, the name itself comes from a decidedly non-math source. It's a variation on the title of a 1964 *Twilight Zone* episode.

Here is the Rod Serling intro for *The Number 12 Looks Just Like You:* "Given the chance, what young girl wouldn't happily exchange a plain face for a lovely one? What girl could refuse the opportunity to be beautiful? For want of a better estimate, let's call it the year 2000. At any rate, imagine a time in the future where science has developed the means of giving everyone the face and body he dreams of. It may not happen tomorrow, but it happens now, in *The Twilight Zone*."

Signature song: *Gallery Of Thrills*
Insight song: *Like A Cat*

N.W.A.

The most famous acronym in music history. (All apologies to ELO). This Compton, California, quintet invented gangsta rap and brought it to the masses. The letters stand for Niggas With Attitude. They were a short-lived, but legendary, band that spawned world-class rap acts who are active to this day.

Signature song: *Straight Outta Compton*
Insight songs: *Dope Man, Express Yourself*

O

OASIS

As huge fans of The Beatles, brothers Noel and Liam Gallagher set out to be the perfect progression of British rock and roll. And that's exactly what these blokes play, good old-fashioned rock music. Like The Beatles, emotions ran high. As a result, the band split up before achieving so much more they were capable of. For a comparison, Oasis lasted eighteen years and recorded seven studio albums. The Beatles lasted eight years, and recorded twelve albums, thirteen EPs and twenty-two singles.

It's hard not to think of The Beatles when listening to, or discussing Oasis. Even their name has significance to their idol band. They named themselves in part after the Oasis Leisure Centre in Swindon, England, where The Beatles once played.

Signature songs: *Wonderwall, Rock-n-Roll Star*
Insight songs: *Underneath The Sky, Part Of The Queue, Acquiesce, Falling Down, Hello*

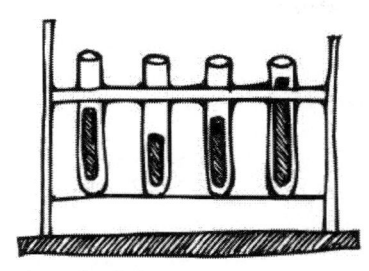

OINGO BOINGO

Before composer Danny Elfman was swinging his baton around for *Batman* and *Spider-man*, he wrote and performed the music for his brother's fantasy film, *Forbidden Zone*.

In 1972, Richard Elfman formed a theatre troupe called the Mystic Knights of the Oingo Boingo. The first part of the name was taken from the *Amos 'n' Andy* series that involved a secret society called the Mystic Knights of the Sea. Additionally, Oingo Boingo is Swahili for "thinking while dancing." A secret society of deep dancers, in other words.

By 1979, Richard's little brother, Danny, was leading the group, and was recruited for the cult classic movie. A year later, the band signed a deal with I.R.S. Records, and dropped the first part of the name, becoming Oingo Boingo.

Later still, and only for one final studio album in 1994, they shortened their name to simply, Boingo. They broke up soon after, but not before performing one last show in Hollywood on Halloween night 1995. That must have been one hell of a send-off for fans. The double album is one of the best live performances ever recorded.

In addition to many other collaborations with Tim Burton, Danny Elfman is the singing voice of Jack Skellington, and composed the songs and score for *The Nightmare Before Christmas*.

(Jack's speaking voice was performed by Chris Sarandon, best known for his role as Prince Humperdink in the 1987 Rob Reiner film, *The Princess Bride*.)

Signature songs: *Weird Science, Dead Man's Party*

Insight songs: *Insanity, Skin, Long Breakdown, Where Do My Friends Go? Elevator Man, Goodbye Goodbye, Just Another Day*

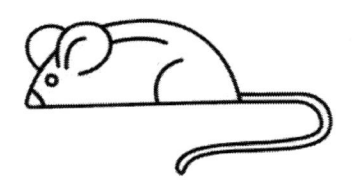

OF MICE AND MEN

This band hails from Costa Mesa, California, although they have roots in Columbus, Ohio. Even though they play pretty freakin' hard rock now, they've actually tamed over the years. Early work should be considered hardcore.

As far as their band name goes, I have one word - Steinbeck. However, Steinbeck's famous novella, for which this band was named, was actually a line in the Robert Burns poem "To a Mouse." The poem is indeed about a mouse, but the book is about two migrant workers displaced by the Great Depression.

Signature songs: *Would You Still Be There?, Second And Sebring*

Insight song: *Obsolete*

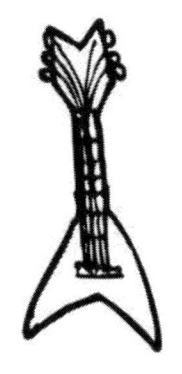

THE OFFSPRING

Half formed from the defunct band Manic Substantial, The Offspring described feeling like they had become the product of a warped society. A 1987 horror movie called *The Offspring* felt right for them.

Known for calling out the status quo, The Offspring always manages to save room on each album for humor. The only thing better than a good song is a good joke in a good song.

Also, they performed the theme song for *Sharknado*, but you'll notice that it is neither listed as a signature song, nor an insight song.

Signature songs: *Self Esteem, Come Out And Play, Pretty Fly For A White Guy*

Insight songs: *Me & My Old Lady, Session, Bad Habit, Spare Me The Details, Worst Hangover Ever*

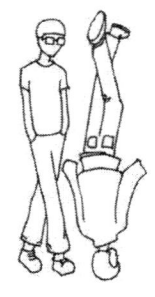

OK GO

Bandmates Damian Kulash and Tim Nordwind had an art teacher in high school that would explain to the class what he wanted them to do, and then would then say, "Okay, go!" The phrase suited the duo's musical style and ambition. The Chicago band is known mostly for having, hands down, the best music videos in the business. Hands down. Go check out a video, any video. You'll be amazed.

Signature song: *Upside Down & Inside Out*
Insight song: *Get Over It*

ONEREPUBLIC
Beginning in Colorado Springs, Colorado, this band started out as Republic but due to copyright issues made it OneRepublic. (They're pop rock superstars if you didn't know.)
Signature songs: *Counting Stars, Love Runs Out*
Insight song: *Wherever I Go*

ONE DIRECTION
Harry Styles has said in an interview that he thought up the name because it sounded good and had no idea what it meant beyond that. (They're even bigger pop superstars if you didn't know.)
Signature songs: *What Makes You Beautiful, History, Perfect*
Insight songs: *Change Your Ticket, Stockholm Syndrome*

OOKLA THE MOC
This is actually a pretty cool name for a reggae band from Hawaii. It comes from a character in the eighties Saturday morning cartoon *Thundarr the Barbarian*. In the cartoon, the creature was known as Ookla The Mok, with a *K*. I guess that name was taken. (Spoiler alert, it was.)
Signature song: *Hell Fire*
Insight song: *Spliff Mood*

OOKLA THE MOK

Yup, this is the band that got a jump on the letter *K*. They formed in 1988, nearly ten years before the Moc's. They most famously wrote and performed the theme song for Disney's show, *Filmore!*, with a quirky style that actually has a name. *Filk* music celebrates nerd culture with a nod to the horror scene as well. The Mok's sound like They Might Be Giants, just with a bigger comic book collection.

Signature songs: *Home, Super Powers*
Insight song: *Doctor Octopus*

OPERATION IVY

Code name of the first US nuclear bomb tests in the Bikini Islands. This punk band from Berkeley was one of the first ska influenced acts to gain traction. They wanted a name that sounded original but had a hidden meaning. Operation Ivy was discarded by another local band, so they took it.

Signature song: *Knowledge*
Insight song: *Bad Town*

OPETH

In the 1972 Wilbur Smith novel, *The Sunbird*, Opet (no *h*), is the name of an ancient lost city on the Moon. This band is from just a little further

away in Stockholm. (Just kidding, Sweden.)
Opeth rocks so hard that you might call them a metal band. However, they regularly incorporate elements of jazz, blues, and even folk music. Metal with breathers. Hence the *h*, maybe.
Signature songs: *In My Time Of Need, Sorceress*
Insight song: *Coil*

OUR LADY PEACE

These rock musicians are from Toronto, Canada, and the ninth best-selling Canadian act in history (behind Avril Lavigne, Diana Krall, Nickelback, Sarah McLachlan, The Tragically Hip, Michael Bublé, Shania Twain, and Celine Dion). They play alternative rock with great harmonies and the name, "Our Lady Peace," is the title of the Mark Van Doren poem about World War II.
Signature songs: *Innocent, Clumsy*
Insight song: *Superman's Dead*

THE OUTFIELD

This English trio played straight-up pop music in the seventies under the name, Sirius B. However, their style didn't fit the punk scene in London, so they broke up. A few years later, this time in the east part of town (which makes a difference, trust me), they re-banded under the moniker, Baseball Boys. CBS Records wanted them for an American audience but suggested that Baseball Boys

sounded too tongue-in-cheek. They kept with the baseball theme and recorded their debut album as The Outfield.
Signature songs: *Your Love, Better Than Nothing*
Insight songs: *Shelter Me, Long Way Home*

OWL CITY
Adam Young has offered competing stories about why he named his solo act Owl City. However, in his blog he mentions once reading a short story by Ambrose Bierce called, *An Occurrence at Owl Creek Bridge*. He reported that the story had a profound influence on him and that naming his band Owl City is a reminder that state of mind is everything.
Signature songs: *Fireflies, Good Time*
Insight song: *Coming After You*

P

PANIC! AT THE DISCO
This band was started at Bishop Gorman High School in Las Vegas by two members who aren't even in the band anymore. They recruited a few more musicians and their demos got the attention of Fall Out Boy's Pete Wentz, whose new label, Fueled By Ramen, was looking for their first band to sign. Panic! At The Disco launched that label to the stars with their debut album, 2005's *A Fever You Can't Sweat Out*.

Rumor is that the name came from a Smiths song called "Panic." The truth according to, now sole member, Brendon Ure is that he "lifted it wholesale" from an indie band called Name Taken. Their song, "Panic," has the lyric: "Panic at the disco, sat back and took it so slow".

Signature songs: *I Write Sins Not Tragedies, Victorious, High Hopes*
Insight songs: *Roaring 20s, Folkin' Around*

PAPA ROACH
They were just kids in Vacaville, California, (northeast of San Francisco) when they chose the name Papa Roach. Other bands they liked had what they considered to be terrible names. Examples being Korn and Primus. So, they set out to find a terrible name. Front man Jacoby Shaddix

had a grandfather with the last name Roach and suggested they use that in some way. Boom! They had it, a truly terrible name, Papa Roach.
Signature song: *Last Resort*
Insight song: *Gravity*

PARADISE LOST
Halifax, England, is a super industrial area, and seems like the type of place that could produce a heavy band like Paradise Lost. These guys were one of the first gothic/doom/metal bands forming in 1988. Their name is taken from the John Milton poem, *Paradise Lost*. Furthermore, this band named their debut album, *Lost Paradise*.
Signature song: *Beneath Broken Earth*
Insight song: *Enchantment*

PAT TODD & THE RANK OUTSIDERS
The song "Rank Outsiders" first appeared on the Lazy Cowgirls 1999 album of the same name. You can't be more of an outsider than a rank outsider. Pat connected early on with the castaway culture that came out of the seventies and early eighties. His music can be either sweetly romantic or savagely cynical, and occasionally both at the same time, which isn't easy.
Signature songs: *Took A Wrong Turn, Somewhere Down The Line*
Insight songs: *Bang Bang & Then You're Dead, Sugar Coated Love*

PEARL JAM

This band, not surprisingly, has some mystery behind its name, but a recent interview with Eddie Vedder finally clarified the subject. Somewhat.

When the band first formed in Seattle they named themselves Mookie Blaylock, after a famed NBA point guard who finished his career with the Golden State Warriors. The band eventually changed that name to avoid any legal issues but used Mookie's jersey number, Ten, as the title of their debut album.

At first, the band selected just the name Pearl, which had a few meanings for them. "Pearling" or "to pearl" is a surfing term that means to dip the nose of the surfboard beneath the water. This usually results in a wipeout. Pearl is also the name of Eddie Vedder's great-grandmother.

However, Eddie once told *Rolling Stone* about a fictitious aunt named Pearl, who made peyote jam. He ultimately revealed that it was really his interest in the actual formation of a pearl that contributed to the band's identity. A pearl is a smooth object created over time inside a creature using an irritant.

The band went to New York City in 1991 as Pearl and came back with the Jam after witnessing many Neil Young jam sessions. They've always been known as a "jam band" so it was probably an easy sell once someone referred to a jam session as a "Pearl Jam."

Is the band aware that their name also sounds like a

reference to semen? Yes. Yes, they are aware of it.
Signature songs: *Even Flow, Corduroy, Jeremy*
Insight songs: *Indifference, Elderly Woman Behind The Counter In A Small Town, Alone*

PENNYWISE

Manhattan Beach, California, is home to these Stephen King fans. When they formed their punk rock band in 1988, the novel *It* was less than two years old, and still scaring the crap out of adults and kids alike. The evil child eating monster calls himself Pennywise, the dancing clown.

Signature songs: *Same Old Story, Fuck Authority*
Insight song: *Divine Intervention*

PHOENIX

Surprise! These guys are from Versailles, France. The small hamlet west of Paris is also home to one of the most ornate palaces ever built in Europe. Constructed by Louis XIV with golden gates, eight square kilometers of maze-like gardens framing huge reflecting pools and great open ovals of grass, Versailles was the royal residence for over a century.

The band name was taken from the 1997 Daft Punk instrumental song "Phoenix". Remember, Daft Punk is also a French band, the biggest French band in history as it happens. Phoenix is number two.

Signature songs: *Trying To Be Cool, Lisztomania, 1901*
Insight song: *Identical*

PHISH

Even though the drummer is Jon Fishman, and his nickname is indeed Fish, the band's name is an onomatopoeia of the sound a brush makes on a snare drum, "phshhh." The band formed at the University of Vermont in Burlington, but have since made the whole planet their home. In fact, they picked up the mantel where Grateful Dead left off. Their live shows have become events, and there is an entire Phish culture. Even the "Shakedown Street" style of parking lot tailgate gatherings echoes the Grateful Dead community.

Signature songs: *Billy Breathes, Bouncing Around The Room*
Insight song: *Slave To The Traffic Light*

PINK FLOYD

This band played around London under the name Tea Set, among others, before settling on a suggestion by founder and lead vocalist Syd Barrett. They performed as The Pink Floyd Sound, a reference to two blues greats from Georgia, Pink Anderson and Floyd "Dipper Boy" Council. They eventually dropped the words on either end and became, simply, Pink Floyd.

Start Me Up

One of the most commercially successful and influential bands in history, Pink Floyd is known for having three distinct eras, each led by a different band member. Syd was the driving force behind the band's first album, *The Piper at the Gates*. Soon after, he had to leave the band due to mental instability. Bassist Roger Waters then took over creative control, including lyric writing and lead vocals. He is responsible for eleven albums including *Dark Side of the Moon*, *Wish You Were Here*, and their seminal concept double album *The Wall*. Waters's last album with the band was called *The Final Cut*, and should be considered more bricks in *The Wall*. Sides D and E, if you will.

When Waters left the band, guitarist David Gilmour led the two remaining band members, Nick Mason and Richard Wright, into the band's third movement. With albums like *Momentary Lapse of Reason* and *The Division Bell*, Floyd proved that they still had something worthy to share.

Pink Floyd's final studio album, *The Endless River,* was released after Richard Wright's death. A fitting farewell that even includes unreleased audio of Wright playing a pipe organ, and songs that are meant to take listeners on a tour de force of Pink Floyd's epic career. A self-made tribute that some critics found tacky, but I love it. Few bands get this kind of closure.

Signature songs: *Comfortably Numb, Another Brick in the Wall, Us and Them*
Insight songs: *Dogs, Pigs, Sheep*

PLAIN WHITE T'S

For lead singer Tom Higgenson, the band name refers to favorite albums of his where band members were wearing plain white tee shirts on the covers. The trio became a quartet in Lanford, Illinois, a suburb of Chicago, and grew their buzz in basement parties with their power/pop/punk vibe.

Signature songs: Hey There Delilah, Rhythm Of Love
Insight song: Should Have Gone To Bed

THE POLICE

Drummer Stuart Copeland was born in America but his father, a CIA officer, had to move the family to Egypt. After college in California, he moved to London where he came up with the iconic band name after a short solo stint as Klark Kent. He corralled guitarist Andy Summers and they met Sting shortly after. Legend has it that Stuart's interest in his father's profession led him to choose an authoritative sounding band identity.

Signature songs: Roxanne, King of Pain, Every Breath You Take
Insight songs: Synchronicity I and II

POWERMAN 5000

Front man Michael David Cummings, aka Spider One, is the younger brother of Rob

Zombie. His Boston based band takes its name from seventies era Marvel comic book hero Luke Cage, aka Power Man. They added the 5000 for flair.
Signature songs: *When Worlds Collide, Super Villains*
Insight songs: *Do Your Thing, Time Bomb*

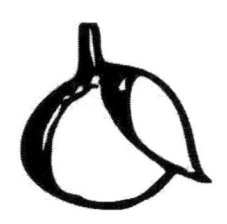

THE PRESIDENTS OF THE UNITED STATES OF AMERICA

While Nirvana and Soundgarden were enjoying super-stardom, this plucky Seattle trio didn't even use all the strings on their instruments, nor did they have a band name. It is said that they would call themselves a different name at the end of each show, as in, "Thank you! Good night! We're Pure Frosting!"

Near the end of 1993, they had a tremendous response to "Thank you! Good night! We're The Presidents of the United States of America!" They went on to record a ten-song cassette called *Froggystyle*, which got them a deal for their debut album, which then sold over three million copies in two years.
Signature songs: *Lump, Kitty, Peaches*
Insight songs: *Tiki God, Tube Amplifier*

THE POSTAL SERVICE

This group is the collaboration of musicians from the bands Dntel and Death Cab for Cutie along with child actress turned singer, Jenny Lewis. They sent each other tapes through the mail as they pieced

together their one and only album, *Give Up*. The band was named after the very institution that made its creation possible, The Postal Service.
Signature songs: *Such Great Heights, Clark Gable*
Insight song: *The District Sleeps Alone Tonight*

PUSCIFER

Pronounced Puss-ifer, (like a devil cat), this band started as a side project for the first episode of HBO's *Mr. Show,* a fictional group that actually began life as, Umlaut. Since Puscifer is the closest thing Maynard James Keenan has to a solo project, it's based at his home and vineyard in Jerome, Arizona. With a once revolving lineup, the group now seems to have settled on the trio of Maynard, Carina Round, and Mat Mitchel.

Maynard James Keenan, possibly the world's greatest rock singer, (TOOL, A Perfect Circle), explains that Puscifer is, "Simply a playground for the various voices in my head. Where my Id, Ego, and Anima all come together to exchange cookie recipes."

With such a sophomoric name for their group, and releases titled, *"V" is for Vagina*, and *Money Shot*, it's tempting to write them off as a joke band, but their music is at the forefront of innovation. Their fourth album, *Existential Reckoning*, was the best release of 2020. (Sorry Parov Stelar, *Voodoo Sonic* was a close second.)

Signature songs: *Vagina Mine, The Remedy*
Insight songs: *Grey Area, UPGrade, Galileo*

Q

QUEEN
This London band was originally called Smile, but Freddie Mercury chose, Queen because, according to him, it was immediate, unusual, and open to all sorts of interpretations. Of course, they were aware that it was a slang term for homosexual, but Freddie said that was "…just one face of it."
Signature songs: *Killer Queen, Bohemian Rhapsody, We Will Rock You*
Insight song: *Fat Bottom Girls*

QUEENS OF THE STONE AGE
According to California guitarist and lead singer, Josh Homme, "Rock should be heavy enough for the boys and sweet enough for the girls… Kings would be too macho." Their music and their name is just that.
Signature song: *Do It Again*
Insight songs: *Feet Don't Fail Me, The Way You Used To Do*

QUEENSRŸCHE
When this band from Bellingham chose their name, they were inspired by one of their own songs, "Queens Of The Reich". They messed with the spelling, added an umlaut, and Queensrÿche was born.

Signature song: *Silent Lucidity*
Insight song: *Last Time In Paris*

QUIET RIOT
Briefly known as Little Women, these Los Angeles headbangers changed their name after a conversation with Status Quo front man, Rick Parfitt. Rick mentioned that he would like to name a band Quite Right but, with his heavy British accent, the band heard it as Quiet Riot. An oxymoron that rhymed was just too good to pass up. Their name was changed on the spot.
Signature song: *Bang Your head, Cum On Feel The Noize*
Insight song: *Slick Black Cadillac*

R

RADIOHEAD

From Abingdon, England, the band was signed to Parlophone Records, but they were asked to change their name from On A Friday to something else. They were given two weeks to do it and chose to name themselves after the song "Radio Head" from the Talking Heads 1986 album, *True Stories*. The explanation given was that it was the least annoying song on the record.

Signature song: *Creep*
Insight song: *Jigsaw Falling Into Place* (Thumbs Down Version)

RAGE AGAINST THE MACHINE

Despite rumors of a certain orange van, this band got their name in an even more nefarious fashion. You see, Zack de la Rocha was in a band called Inside Out, and they were already putting stuff together on a demo cassette. They were going to call their debut album, *Rage Against the Machine*.

Zack heard that name and knew at once it was too good to be wasted as the title of an album. He thought it was, "The sickest band name in the history of band names." He talked his buddies into jumping ship and stealing the name for themselves.

They were lucky enough to get a spot as a local act opening for Public Enemy in San Luis Obispo, California. When they were introduced to the crowd as Rage and the Machine, Zack stormed onto the stage, grabbed the mic out of one of the rapper's hands, and screamed, "Rage AGAINST the Machine!" That was the show that changed everything for them.

Signature song: *Bulls On Parade*
Insight song: *Pistol Grip Pump*

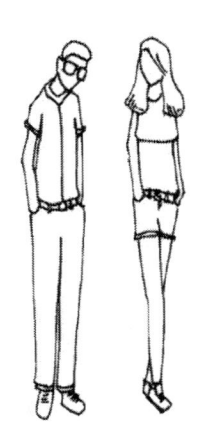

RAINER MARIA

This is a power trio from Madison, Wisconsin, who later relocated to Brooklyn. They play emo rock with often biting and confessional lyrics.

They named their band after the German poet, Rainer Maria Rilke. This was, in part, because her (professional) name was both feminine and masculine. The band had two lead singers in the early days, one girl, Caithlin De Marrais, and one boy, Kaia Fischer.

Signature songs: *Ears Ring, Catastrophe*
Insight songs: *Artificial Light, Breakfast Of Champions*

RASCAL FLATTS

This country trio is from Columbus, and played without a name until their audience began asking for one. They took suggestions and, at one point, an older gentleman is said to have approached them. He told them about an area outside of Salisbury, Missouri. Flatlands that were occupied by horse thieves and the like back during the Civil War. Locals called that area the rascal flats, and he always thought it would make a cool band name.

Signature song: *What Hurts The Most*
Insight song: *Stand*

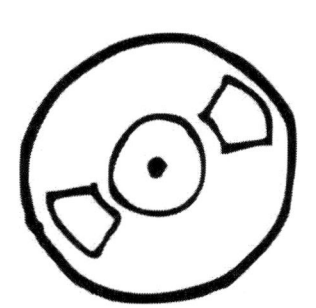

RATT

RATT's origins began back in 1973, in Hollywood. Stephen Pearcy founded a band called Firedome, which broke up a year later. So he started again with a band he called, Crystal Pystal, which became Buster Cherry, which became Mickey Ratt by 1976. They played under the name Micky Ratt for five years, pressing the single, "Dr. Rock" and giving it away at shows. ("Drivin' On E" was the song on the flip side.) They didn't shorten their name to RATT until they got a record deal in 1981.

Signature songs: *Round And Round, Way Cool Jr.*
Insight song: *Slip Of That Lip*

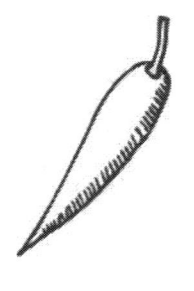

RED HOT CHILI PEPPERS

When starting out in Los Angeles, Anthony Kiedis and company called themselves, Tony Flow and the Miraculously Majestic Masters of Mayhem. (Yikes! I'll take Hot Tuna.) Anthony recalled that jazz bands of the fifties were always called the red hot something-or-other. Or something something and the chili peppers. They simply put the two concepts together and liked how it sounded.

Signature songs: Under The Bridge, Higher Ground, Life Is Beautiful

Insight songs: Around The World, I Like Dirt, Aquatic Mouth Dance

RED JUMPSUIT APPARATUS

Started by childhood friends in Middleburg, Florida, in 2001, this emo band didn't become official until they added three more members two years later. They picked their name by posting random words on a wall. "One hundred percent arbitrary," says co-founder and lead singer Ronnie Winter. They wanted something flashy and memorable. All they had to do was wait until it presented itself.

Signature songs: Face Down, Your Guardian Angel

Insight songs: Is This The Real World?, Pen And Paper

REEL BIG FISH

Not just a ska band, but a super vocal ska band with tighter vocals than Kansas. They started out as a high school rock trio, but discovered ska, and started developing a horn section. It took a while, and has had a historical rotation. In fact, only front man Aaron Barnett remains from the original line-up.
They took their band name from an early demo song, which is now known as, "Return of the Mullet."
Signature songs: She Has A Girlfriend Now, Beer, Sell Out, Take On Me *(cover)*
Insight songs: New York New York *(cover)*, Everyone Else Is An Asshole, S.R. *(live)*

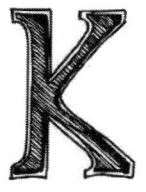

RELIENT K

Somewhere in Canton, Ohio, is the Plymouth Reliant K that these Christian rockers named themselves after. Also, they have a really great Christmas album.
Signature song: Who I Am Hates Who I've Been
Insight song: Sadie Hawkins Dance

R.E.M.

The most famous band from Athens, even though the B-52s beat them to the scene. According to myth, Michael

Stipe was flipping through the dictionary in hopes of striking on a band name. The definition of the acronym, Rapid Eye Movement, which refers to the most optimum stage of sleep, was of no consequence to him. It stood out, and that's what Michael was looking for.

There is a theory that R.E.M. is indeed a secret acronym meaning Remember Every Moment, but I believe Michael Stipe and Co. wouldn't hide something so elegant. It's not that they can't keep a secret, it's just that they are poets, and romantics to boot. No way they keep something that poignant to themselves.

Signature songs: *Radio Free Europe, The One I Love, Stand, Orange Crush, Losing My Religion, It's The End of The World As We Know It (And I Feel Fine)*

Insight songs: *Untitled (11th track on the Green album), Nightswimming, These Days, So. Central Rain, Maps And Legends*

RIGHT SAID FRED

It's funny to me that this band is neighbors with R.E.M. because it was Right Said Fred's biggest hit, "I'm Too Sexy" that knocked R.E.M.'s biggest hit, "Losing My Religion" out of the top spot on Billboard's Modern Rock chart after an eight-week run in the spring of 1991. Another interesting connection is that they both have an album titled *Up*.

Brothers Richard and Fred Fairbrass, who make up the band, were fans of the 1962 Bernard Cribbins novelty

song, "Right Said Fred." But there's more to it than that, with a thick enough English accent, and I mean a nice Dick Van Dyke in *Mary Poppins* as Burt the chimney sweep kind of accent, the name Richard sounds like, right said. (Like I said, you'd have to have a Cockney accent so thick the Artful Dodger himself couldn't understand you.) Anyway, with this accent, the brothers' names, Richard/Fred would sound like Right Said Fred.
Signature song: *I'm Too Sexy*
Insight song: *You're My Mate*

THE ROLLING STONES
As the story goes, the London based boys were about to audition for a record company and the name was blurted out by Brian Jones, who knew it as the title of a Muddy Waters song. The Stones are, at their core, a blues band after all. There are many versions of this story, some that include that very Muddy Waters record being in the room.
Signature songs: *Satisfaction, Brown Sugar*
Insight songs: *All of the Exile On Main Street album*

THE ROMANTICS
It is said that this band formed on Valentine's Day. It was definitely in Detroit and in 1977, but the rest is pure theory. I get it. I mean, what else were they going to call themselves? Heart was already taken. So was Lovin' Spoonful.
The real story is that their name came from an article about

Bryan Ferry in *CREEM* magazine. The word romantic was used more than once to describe his songwriting and his performance style. Jimmy Marinos was inspired by that notion and named his new band, The Romantics.

Signature songs: *What I Like About You, Talking In Your Sleep*
Insight song: *One In A Million*

THE ROMNAY RYE

This is the title of George Borrow's 1857 sequel to *Lavengro*. (I know, right? That's a rabbit hole I just spent the last thirty minutes spelunking.) Anyway, this band is from Long Beach, California; the only place that can still get away with calling the state Cali. (They'll like that joke because it's true, and they still do.) These five bearded boys play indie/folk music, and they're so good, even Counting Crows have covered some of their work.

Signature song: *(Untitled) Love Song*
Insight song: *Old Soul*

ROXY MUSIC

Band founder, Bryan Ferry, was terminated from his teaching job at a "girls" school in 1970 because he held record listening sessions. He advertised for a keyboardist to collaborate with and tried out unsuccessfully for the lead singing position in Crimson King. However, the band was impressed with Bryan and eventually helped his band get a contract with E.G. Records.

The first person to apply for the position was saxophonist Andy Mackay, who did own a synthesizer that Ferry talked friend Brian Eno into playing. They were all interested in avant-garde, progressive rock.

By the end of the year, they found Roger Bunn for guitar duties and drummer Dexter Lloyd. Their debut album was out less than a year later.

The name Roxy came from Ferry and Mackey listing old movie theatres. Roxy sounded like "faded glamour." They added the "Music" after it was discovered that an American band had named themselves Roxy.

Signature songs: *More Than This, Jealous Guy, Love Is The Drug*

Insight song: *Virginia Plain*

RUN-DMC

The fathers of new school rap came from Hollis, Queens, New York. Joseph Simmons had the nickname Run due to his record scratching abilities. Darryl McDaniels was known as D.M.C.—before that, he was known as Grandmaster Get High. The band's third member is Jason "Jam Master Jay" Mizell. He's the band's official recording and performing DJ.

Signature songs: *Walk This Way, Tricky, My Adidas*

Insight song: *Rock Box*

THE RUNNAWAYS

This all female group fought against the stereotype that they were nothing more than a Los Angeles sexploitation act, all the while feeding that very image, including with their band name. Everything about them screams, JAILBAIT on purpose. They beat the system by letting their solid punk rock speak for itself. Now the women enjoy their exalted place in rock history.

Signature song: *Cherry Bomb*
Insight song: *Blackmail*

RUSH

Late drummer John Rutsey met schoolmate Alex Lifeson at St. Paschal's in 1963. They formed a band called The Projection. By 1968, they met bassist Jeff Jones who was replaced soon after by Geddy Lee, who had a mysterious look, a unique voice, and a level of proficiency on the bass that wowed onlookers.

The band worked at their craft and got their first gig in May 1971, in the basement of St. Theodore of Canterbury Anglican Church in North York, Toronto. The only problem was they hadn't chosen a name for the band yet. During a brainstorming session, John's brother suggested Rush. It fit the band's up-tempo approach perfectly.

Due to health issues, John had to quit the band after their 1974 debut album was released. The timing was problematic because the band was set to tour America two weeks later. His replacement was Neil Peart, who just happened to be one of the best drummers on planet Earth. He saved the tour, and his inclusion cemented the legendary trio we know today.

Signature songs: *Freewill, Fly By Night, Tom Sawyer, Spirit Of The Radio*

Insight songs: *Natural Science, Spindrift, Working Them Angels, Between the Wheels, The Body Electric*

S

SAVAGE GARDEN

A duo from Queensland, Australia, that sold over twenty million copies of their debut album. Too bad they only released one more after that. The mid-nineties could have used more pop to break up the grunge wave.

Their name was taken from the 1985 Anne Rice novel *The Vampire Lestat*, where she writes: "No one is safe from nature's savagery, not even the innocent. Gabrielle envisions a time when the savage garden will overtake civilizations and destroy it."

Signature songs: *I Want You, Affirmation*
Insight songs: *Chained To You, Carry On Dancing*

SAVE FERRIS

As in, "Bueller? Bueller? Bueller?" This band was a part of the ska-punk scene in Southern California in the mid-nineties. Their lead singer, Monique Powell, sounds just like Gwen Stefani.

The movie *Ferris Bueller's Day Off* was the obvious inspiration for their name. The words "SAVE FERRIS" were written on a water tower in the film.

"What if you need a favor some day from Ferris Bueller? Then where will you be, huh? You heartless wench!" – Guy holding donations can with the words "SAVE FERRIS" written on it.

Signature songs: *I Know, The World Is New*
Insight song: *Goodbye*

666 SAY ANYTHING

Hard rockers from Los Angeles who chose to share the name of the famous 1989 John Cusack film. But, of course, the words mean so much more. They have a lot of power as a band name. Plus, it's ironic that people think of a romantic comedy movie from the eighties because these guys are super hardcore.

Signature songs: *Shiksa, Have Everyone*
Insight song: *Six Six Six*

SEETHER

Some origin cities come as a surprise. This one might. Actually, everything about this band is interesting. The group is from Pretoria, South Africa. Pretoria is in the northern part of the country, in the province of Gauteng. Serving as one of three capital cities, Pretoria serves as the seat of the executive branch of government.

The band enjoyed success as Saron Gas, but when they relocated to the USA they changed the name, for the obvious reason that it sounds just like Sarin Gas. Which, come to think of it, isn't a terrible name. It might even be better than Seether. That is, unless Seether has a cool origin story and, frankly, I could go either way. I believe it depends largely on how much you like Veruca Salt.

"Seether" is the name of the first, and biggest, single by Veruca Salt, a band with a name that's also a pop culture reference. Not nearly as subtle as Seether, but we'll get to them later.

Seether struck gold when they were asked to open for Evanescence. Amy Lee took their song "Broken" and did what Amy Lee does ... makes everything better.

Signature songs: *Broken, Remedy, Fire Again*
Insight songs: *Dangerous, Pass Slowly*

SEVEN MARY THREE

This one is funny, especially for Gen X. The band name is taken from the 1970s hit TV show, *CHiPs*. Character Jon Baker's Highway Patrol call sign is 7Mary3. His partner, Francis "Ponch" Poncherello, is 7Mary4.

The band comes from Williamsburg, Virginia, and season their modern rock with country spice. I would say they land somewhere between Lynyrd Skynyrd and Clutch.

Signature songs: *Cumbersome, Lucky*
Insight song: *Water's Edge*

SILVERCHAIR

This teenage Australian trio frequently changed their name. They were once called Innocent Criminals, The George Constanza Trio, and Short Elvis. Silverchair just happened to be the handle they were using when they hit it big with a record contract and a debut album that sold around the world. They intended to change their name again but, since the band now had a brand to protect, they just kept it.

Side note: Inside their debut album, *Frogstomp*, are the words, "All apologies to Toad the Wet Sprocket."

Signature songs: *Tomorrow, Faultline*
Insight songs: *Shade, Suicidal Dream*

SIMPLE MINDS

This band name was taken from the third verse of the David Bowie song "The Jean Genie," which was the first single from his 1972 album *Ziggy Stardust*.

Simple Minds coalesced in Glasgow in 1977, which seems like a seminal year in band formations. They were new wave but had a post-punk streak, and were most famous for their performance of "Don't You (Forget About Me)," recorded specifically for the 1985 John Hughes film, *The Breakfast Club*.

Signature songs: *Don't You (Forget About Me), Alive And Kicking, Glittering Prize*
Insight song: *Speed Your Love To Me*

SIMPSONS SUBSECTION:
This TV show has eleven bands named after it. (That I know of!)

EVERGREEN TERRACE
Metalcore band from Jacksonville, Florida.
FALL OUT BOY
Rock/Punk band from Wilmette, Illinois.
HOT ROD CIRCUIT
Indie rock band from Auburn, Alabama.
I VOTED FOR KODOS
Ska/Punk band from Madison, Wisconsin.
JEBEDIAH
Alternative rock band from Perth, Australia.
JEBUS
Quirky rockers from Manchester, England.
JIMBO JONES
Crazy Norwegian unorthodox rockers.
MAD MARGE AND THE STONECUTTERS
Female led punk rockers from Victorville, California.
MR. PLOW
Metalheads from Alvin, Texas.
OKILLY DOKILLY
More metalheads, but these guys are from Phoenix and they all dress like Ned Flanders, complete with real mustaches. It's hilarious.
THRICE
Alternative rockers from Irvine, California.

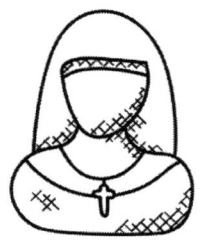

SISTER HAZEL

First of all, I want to get it out there that super fans of this band are known as Hazel Nuts and that's hysterical. Sister Hazel Williams was a well-known missionary who ran a homeless shelter in the band's hometown of Gainesville, Florida. They named their band for her.
Sister Hazel's southern rock sound helped them separate from other alternative bands of the nineties, and their breakout album was the sophomore effort, ...*Somewhere More Familiar.*
Signature song: *All For You*
Insight song: *Superman*

THE SLITS

This seventies London punk band was made up of all girls with a lot to prove. Primarily, that they could be just as vulgar as the boys. Hence, the biologically suggestive name. The punk rockers actually came together from two different bands, The Flowers Romance and The Castrators.
Signature song: *Typical Girls*
Insight song: *So Tough*

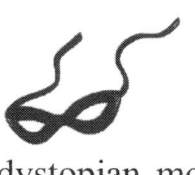

SOYLENT GREEN

Only a hardcore metal band would choose this as their name. It's the title of the 1973 dystopian movie starring Charlton Heston. If you don't know, you really should know.

These guys are from New Orleans, and you can sort of hear that bluesy rock influence somewhere behind all the screaming.
Signature song: *Antioxidant*
Insight song: *It Was Just An Accident*

SQUIRREL NUT ZIPPERS

Squirrel Nut Zippers is the name of an old-timey American caramel candy. Additionally, Nut Zippers became a term for a type of bootleg moonshine.

So, it was quite clever when a newspaper headline in the band's hometown of Chapel Hill, North Carolina read, 'Squirrel Nut Zipper' above the picture of a drunk man who climbed a tree and refused police commands to come down.

Since the sound of this band comes right out of the swing era of the 1930s and 1940s, the name fits perfectly.
Signature songs: *Hell, Put A Lid On It, Karnival Joe* (From *Kokomo)*
Insight songs: *Suits Are Picking Up The Bill, Ghost Of Stephen Foster*

SMASHING PUMPKINS

A small group of bands have a name that was chosen long before there was ever a band. Billy Corgan told Chicago friends in high school that he would one day have a band called Smashing Pumpkins. Billy

stated in an interview that the name suited the band in the end, because they were doomed to be broken.
Signature songs: Today, Bullet With Butterfly Wings
Insight songs: The Celestials, Cyr, The Everlasting Gaze, Tarantula

SMASHMOUTH
Mike Ditka, famed coach of the Chicago Bears, coined the phrase Smash Mouth Football. These San Jose party rockers felt it fit their style of music.
Signature songs: Walking On The Sun, All Star
Insight songs: Diggin' Your Scene, When The Morning Comes, Defeat You

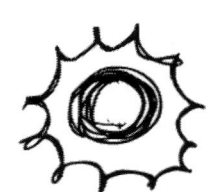

SOUNDGARDEN
In 1983, sculptor Douglas Hollis completed an immersive art experience on the NOAA campus in Seattle. The interactive art project consisted of twelve steel towers, each topped with a weather vane and an organ pipe with complementary tones to one another. The structure is called, *A Sound Garden.* One year later, Chris Cornell and company adapted the name for their new band.

Soundgarden were heroes in the Seattle music scene and achieved global success in 1991 with their third album, *Badmotorfinger.* This was the same year the Seattle sound exploded into every kid's speakers, with Nirvana and Pearl Jam both releasing their breakout albums.

Signature songs: *Outshined, Spoonman, Black Hole Sun*
Insight songs: *Rusty Cage, Attrition, Drawing Flies*

SPANDAU BALLET

Starting out as the house band for the Blitz Kids, under the name The Applause, these mostly rotating London musicians had many other names. In the 1970s, they played as Roots, The Cut, The Makers, and Gentry in addition to their house band persona.

It was friend and writer Robert Elms who suggested Spandau Ballet because he saw it graffitied on a subway wall in Berlin. Spandau is the westernmost borough of Berlin and, as far as I can find, does not have a ballet. It has a citadel, a prison and a BMW Factory, so it must have some ballet, too?

They play romantic electronic music, and their single, "True" is the theme song for the 1984 John Hughes film, *Sixteen Candles*.

Signature songs: *True, Gold*
Insight song: *To Cut A Long Story Short*

STEELY DAN

Annandale-on-Hudson is a hamlet in Red Hook, New York. This band first formed as a duo in 1971. With many line-ups, the group was always able to explore a very jazzy approach to rock.

By the way, Steely Dan is the name of a steam powered dildo in the 1959 William S. Burroughs novel, *Naked Lunch*.

Signature songs: *Do It Again, Reelin' In The Years*
Insight song: *Deacon Blue*

STEPPENWOLF

Steppenwolf is a classic rock Los Angeles band that was at the height of success between 1968 and 1972. Then, everybody left except for lead singer John Kay.

The group lifted their name from the 1927 Hermann Hesse novel, *Der Steppenwolf*. The book wasn't published in English until 1929. Coincidentally, the story is about a homeless man after the stock market crash.

Signature songs: *Born To Be Wild, Magic Carpet Ride*
Insight songs: *Don't Step On The Grass, Sam*

STRAWBERRY ALARM CLOCK

Originally called Three Sixpence, this Glendale, California, band was signed to Uni Records in 1967. The label suggested the a name change to something trippy. The final choice was, in part, an homage to the current hit "Strawberry Fields Forever" by The Beatles.

Signature song: *Incense And Peppermints*
Insight song: *Rainy Day Mushroom Pillow*

STYX

Easily one of the most underrated classic rock bands ever to create music, Styx took their name from the river that separates Earth from the Underworld in Greek mythology. They formed in Chicago in the mid-sixties under the name, Tradewinds. But when they lost a member, it was changed to TW4 (There were 4 left).

When the band was signed to Wooden Nickel Records in 1972, they decided to change their name again. Styx became the frontrunner choice because, according to Dennis DeYoung, "It was the only name nobody hated."

You would think that a band named Styx would be more aggressive but these musicians perfected a sweet and salty sound, where romance was almost always the subject of their songs. The group could rock with the best of them, but could also take it slow like no other band, except Led Zeppelin.

Signature songs: *Come Sail Away, Mr. Roboto, The Best Of Times*

Insight song: *Suite Madame Blue*

SUBHUMANS

This English band is in the punk rock hall of fame and made up of members from two other groups, The Mental and The Stupid Humans. They became Subhumans shortly after Dick Lucas joined the band. This was all much to the chagrin of Bruce Treasure's mom, who wanted to call them The Superhumans.

On most of their albums they spell their name in three little boxes as SUB HUM ANS. I always liked that. It would make a sweet tattoo.
Signature song: *Subvert City*
Insight songs: *Mickey Mouse Is Dead, Rats*

SUGAR RAY
In the early days of playing and rehearsing in Newport Beach, California, the band called themselves, The Tories. In 1986, they changed their name to Shrinky Dinx, and there it stayed for nearly a decade. When they were signed in 1996, the band needed to choose something else to avoid any legal entanglements from Milton Bradley, maker of Shrinky Dinks toys.

Sugar Ray was similarly syllabled, and also an iconic image, so they went with that. They mostly have a funky/pop vibe, but can go metal at times. For real.
Signature songs: *Every Morning, Someday*
Insight songs: *Ten Seconds Down, RPM*

SUPERTRAMP
Who's Your Daddy? was Supertramp's first name. After several rehearsals, and a filmed concert in Munich that culminated in a ten-minute cover of "All Along the Watchtower," they had the first of many member changes. They also decided to change their name to avoid being confused with another London band, Daddy Longlegs.

The band was started by keyboardist Keith Davies, who already had a Dutch backer. The band he'd played in before was dissolved by the wealthy musical entrepreneur, and he was subsequently asked to lead a new group that would showcase his bluesy style. He hired three great musicians but, like many bands before and since, their differing musical tastes would be both a blessing and a curse.

Their name came from the 1908 W. H. Davies book, *Autobiography of a Supertramp*, which is about exactly what it sounds like.

Signature songs: *Take The Long Way Home, Give A Little Bit, The Logical Song*
Insight song: *School*

SYSTEM OF A DOWN

This band name was taken from a poem titled "Victims of a Down" and written by their guitarist, Doran Malakian. The word *victims* seemed too limiting and off-putting, so bassist Shavo Odadjian suggested replacing it with *system*. The group agreed after realizing that their albums would sit in the same section as Slayer's.

Signature song: *Chop Suey*
Insight song: *Bounce*

T

TEARS FOR FEARS

This duo is from Bath, England, and teamed up after their other band, Gratitude, broke up in 1981. Because of that association, Tears For Fears were lumped in with the new wave bands coming from Britain at that time. In reality, their songs are less electronic and more traditional pop rock. With one of the best vocalists around, Roland Orzabal, their songs played to his many strengths and dripped with lyrical pathos.

The band name, as well as much of their debut album's theme, was taken from the 1980 Arthur Janov book, *Prisoners of Pain*.

Signature songs: *Shout, Everybody Wants To Rule The World, Mad World*

Insight song: *Woman In Chains*

TEMPLE OF THE DOG

The band was formed in Seattle in 1990 as a tribute to Andrew Wood, former lead singer of Mother Love Bone, who had recently died of a drug overdose. This supergroup recorded one album.

Chris Cornell, of Soundgarden, formed the band along with members of Mother Love Bone and

Pearl Jam. The name was chosen from a Mother Love Bone song called "Man of Golden Words."
Signature song: *Hunger Strike*
Insight songs: *Wooden Jesus, Reach Down*

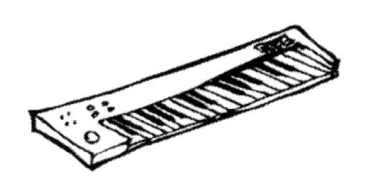

TEN YEARS AFTER

There are two accounts of how this band got their name. Before they got around to Ten Years After, they really got around. Founder Ivan Jay began in 1960 with his group, Ivan Jay and the Jaycats. In 1962, they became Ivan Jay and the Jaymen, which was quickly replaced with The Jaybirds.

When the group moved to London in 1966, and got a manager, (and a keyboard player), they changed their name to Blues Trip. A good name, as it pretty much described their music. However, when they opened for the Bonzo Dog Doo-Dah Band, their biggest gig to date, they were listed as Blues Yard.

Later that year, they finally landed on their established name. One story is that bassist Leo Lyons spotted the name in a magazine article headlined, 'Suez, Ten Years After' (a reference to the crisis in the Suez canal in 1956). The other story is that front man Alvin Lee chose the name to honor his idol, Elvis Presley, who was enjoying the tenth anniversary of his breakout year.

Signature songs: *Rock & Roll To The World, I'd Like To Change The World*
Insight song: *Woke Up This Morning*

THEY MIGHT BE GIANTS

Formed in Lincoln, Massachusetts, but based in Brooklyn. The duo took their name from a 1971 film starring George C. Scott, whose character believes he is Sherlock Holmes. The name, They Might Be Giants, was itself a reference to the fictional character Don Quixote, who pretended that windmills were giants.

Astonishingly, this band has recorded a song every day since 1982. Their *Dial-A-Song* project began in 1983, allowing fans to call daily to hear a new tune over the phone. That number, by the way, is 718-387-6962, but it's usually busy. Thanks to internet, these songs can now also be found on dialasong.com. This effort makes the band the most prolific in history, with available songs numbering deep into the thousands.

Signature songs: *Anna Ng, Istanbul (Not Constantinople)*
Insight songs: *Spy, Boat of Car, Your Racist Friend*

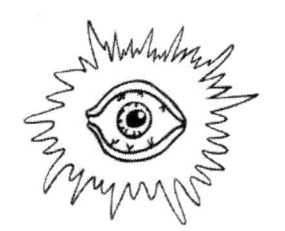

THIRD EYE BLIND

Enter Stephen Jenkins. He earned his English degree from the University of California at Berkeley before becoming a popular San Francisco solo artist. To explore a bigger sound, he pieced together several bands in the mid-nineties before the right combination of musicians fell into place.

He dubbed his rock group Third Eye Blind as a reference

to the metaphysical concept that we all have a mind's eye, which is often and willfully closed.
Signature songs: *Semi-Charmed Life, How's It Going To Be?, Jumper*
Insight song: *Crystal Baller*

THREE DAYS GRACE

Some of the group's members played together in a high school band in Norwood, Ontario. But, back in 1992, they went by the name Groundswell. When school was over, that band broke up. Three ex-members regrouped, moved to Toronto and formed Three Days Grace.

Three Days Grace is a term familiar to college students, who will sometimes hear a professor announce the due date for papers or projects with "three days grace." However, the band developed a different interpretation of the words. According to lead singer Adam Gontier the name is really a challenge: What if you could change your whole life in just three days? Those days would be your own personal three days grace. The group's music reflects this sentiment. It's urgent and tough.

Signature songs: *Never Too Late, Animal I Have Become*
Insight song: *Riot*

THREE DOG NIGHT

While trying to come up with a name that highlighted the unusual fact that the band had three lead singers, the group almost settled on the homoerotic, at best, Tricycle. But Danny Hutton's girlfriend suggested a term used by the Australian Aboriginals to describe how many dogs would be needed to sleep with to keep warm on the colder nights. A two dog night was common, but a three dog night was really getting chilly.

Signature song: *Joy To The World*
Insight song: *Sure As I'm Sittin' Here*

TITUS ANDRONICUS

Titus Andronicus is generally regarded as William Shakespeare's bloodiest work and known to be his first tragedy. (Likely written in collaboration with George Peele and first performed in 1590, give or take a year.)
The band formed in Glen Rock, New Jersey, and play emo punk music. It's a pretty righteous combo. (Think of a way more electric Violent Femmes mixed with a less bluesy Lazy Cowgirls.) Yes, I'm aware that over half of this entry has been in parentheses. Ironically, in my fiction work, (which is mostly what I write), I detest the usage of parenthetical, and never employ such methods of communication, because its design is to pull the reader from the story (albeit for a brief aside), which I think is usually unwanted, seldom humorous, and rarely worth

what you risk in pulling focus from the reader just to satisfy some bit of narrative that couldn't be disseminated through more clever means. However, in writing this collection, I have been liberated of the need to fret over such frivolities, (plus, I can indulge in alliterations, which is frowned upon in fiction.)

While we're on the subject on writing tips, the above paragraph is an absolute CLINIC on proper parenthetical punctuation. (After my editor gets done with it of course. ((And how about that sweet triple alliteration just then, which now gives me the opportunity to illustrate a double parenthetical and its proper punctuation.).)

This one's for you, Marla!
Signature song: *A More Perfect Union*
Insight song: *Dimed Out*

TOAD THE WET SPROCKET

The band began in Santa Barbara, and got the name from a Monty Python sketch called "Rock Notes". In it, Eric Idle announces, "Rex Stardust, lead electric triangle, with Toad the Wet Sprocket has had to have an elbow removed following their recent successful worldwide tour of Finland."

This band achieved near musical perfection with their third album, 1991's *Fear*, which produced their two biggest hits and began a streak of thoughtful rock success that was not only constantly fresh, but familiar at the same time. Their follow-up albums, *Dulcinea* and *Coil,* are wholly underrated.

Signature songs: *All I Want, Walk On The Ocean*
Insight songs: *Nightingale Song, Fall Down, Whatever I Fear*

TOOL

"Tool is exactly what it sounds like, It's a big dick. It's a wrench. We are your tool. Use us as a catalyst in your process of finding out whatever it is you need to find out." –Maynard James Keenan, lead singer. The band was started by a group of mostly film students in Los Angeles in 1989. Early on, they fabricated the story that their band formed because of "lachrymology," a religion that embraces pain and crying as a release. As it turns out, they also made up the dogma.

Signature songs: *Sober, Ænema*
Insight songs: *Pneuma, 7empest, Right In Two, 10,000 Days (Wings for Marie Parts I & II)*

TOP MEN

I'm a sucker for a great movie reference, and this is the best one since, I Don't Know How But They Found Me, back on page 111. "Top men" is one of the lines of dialogue in the 1981 film *Raiders of the Lost Ark*. It's the only answer Indiana Jones is given when he asks who in the U.S. government would be looking after the properties of the newly acquired Arc of the Covenant.

The band is a riot of skilled and saucy electro-sci-fi-funk. They're from Vancouver, which explains why they're so funny, and back their good humor up with some brilliant musicianship.
Signature song: *Drop The Hammer*
Insight song: *Hypersleep*

TOTO
This band wants to make it clear that they are not named after the dog in *Wizard of Oz*. The phrase "In toto" is Latin for "All Encompassing." That expression was written on their demo tapes at a busy Los Angeles studio to keep them from getting lost or used by other bands. The name stuck. The group has a rich classic rock sound with noteworthy harmonies and far-out lyrics.

The band hated the song, "Africa" by the way. Also noteworthy is the fact that their lead vocalist, Joseph Williams, is the son of film composer John Williams.
Signature songs: *Africa, Rosanna,*
Insight song: *St. George And The Dragon*

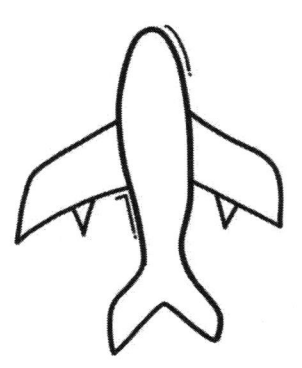

TWENTY-ONE PILOTS
Josh Dunn and Tyler Joseph read an Arthur Miller play in high school, called *All My Sons*. The drama is about a man whose parts company supplies the military during WWII. He discovers that his airplane parts

are faulty and has to decide between sending them out anyway, and possibly causing harm, or holding them back and damaging his company's reputation. When he decides to ship out the bad parts, twenty-one pilots die as a direct result, including his own son.

The homage is a reminder that when we face moral crossroads, we must endeavor to seek the choice that benefits our fellow man, and not just our own interests.

The music this duo produces is brave modern rock, but each song is a new journey musically. They have many looks, and each album is a seminar in songwriting. This is the kind of band that other bands listen to for inspiration.

Signature songs: *Ode To Sleep, Stressed Out, Ride, Lane Boy, Jumpsuit*

Insight songs: *Banditos, Morph, Neon Gravestones*

TWO DOOR CINEMA CLUB

This Irish trio are all film buffs and named themselves after the Tudor Theater in their hometown of Bangor. Their sound is post-punk, which is to say dancy punk.

Signature songs: *Sun, Undercover Martyn, Something Good Can Work*

Insight song: *Not In This Town*

U

U2

I would say that this band is the pride of Dublin, Ireland, but what I discovered when I visited the city is that most people there think Bono is a wanker. Don't get me wrong. They love U2, but Dublin has a thing about keeping people humble.

From 1976 to 1978, the band operated under three different names: The Larry Mullen Band, Feedback, and finally The Hype. One of their friends shamed them into dumping the latter because it was so stupid. They settled on U2 because it was the name of a spy plane, a subway line in East Berlin, and also had an inclusive vibe by sounding like, *you too*. Their music is soulful and rock based, but they have plenty of pop songs.

For the record, U2 only wanted to make their 2014 album, Songs Of Innocence free of charge. They had no idea iTunes was going to include it in an update and download it to all of their users overnight. A lot of people don't know that part of the story.

Signature songs: *With Or Without You, Sunday Bloody Sunday, I Still Haven't Found What I'm Looking For*
Insight songs: *When Love Comes To Town, Raised By Wolves*

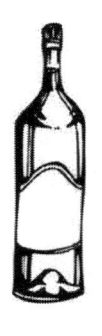

UB40

This band name came courtesy of the Department of Employment in Birmingham, England. When the group formed in the late seventies, they were all unemployed and, therefore, had to fill out a form for Unemployment Benefits. Specifically, Form 40. In other words, they had to submit a weekly UB40. They have a reggae/rock sound, and their biggest hit is a Neil Diamond cover.

Signature song: *Red Red Wine*
Insight song: *Rat In Mi Kitchen*

UGLY KID JOE

This Isla Vista, California, band may look like a bunch of surfers but they play like Slayer. Ugly Kid Joe chose their name to rib the Hollywood band, Pretty Boy Floyd. The video for their hit song "Everything About You" shows the band on a beach, flying a blow-up sex doll as a kite. It's hilarious.

Signature song: *Everything About You*
Insight song: *Hell Ain't Hard To Find*

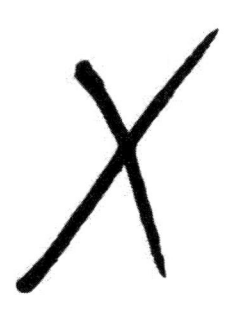

UNDERWORLD

Founding, and only remaining, members Karl Hyde and Rick Smith started out with an edgy electro-quintet called Freur. They recorded an album for CBS Records called *Doot-Doot,* but disbanded when their sophomore effort was withheld. They quickly reformed to score a 1985 horror film, written by Clive Barker and directed by George Pavlou. The film was called *Underworld*, and the band signed with Sire Records under that name.

They released two awesome pop/rock albums before recruiting DJ Darren Emerson and delving deeper into long progressive songs that made single based format songs quaint by comparison. *dubnobasswithmyheadman* did for electronic dance music what Nirvana's *Nevermind* did for alternative music. The once underground techno culture exploded into the mainstream.

The trio became instant legends, a title they proved had not given in haste with follow-up albums, *Second Toughest in the Infants* and *Beaucoup Fish*. Emerson has since stepped back into his solo performances, but Hyde and Smith continued on with numerous acclaimed albums.

Signature songs: *Born Spippy. NUXX, Cowgirl*
Insight songs: *Big Red X, Trimm, Bruce Lee*

URIAH HEEP

Like many late sixties London bands, Uriah Heep played hard rock but always included a little something extra to keep fans guessing. They started out as Hogwash, which is a name I rather like. They then became Spice, got a manager, a record contract, and were recording their first album in the winter of 1969.

That winter in London was heavily focused on the one hundredth anniversary of the death of author Charles Dickens. (By the way, I made that last sentence as long as possible because Dickens was paid a nickel per word back then, which explains his verbose style.) Inspired, the band renamed themselves after a sycophantic character in the Dickens novel, *David Copperfield*.

Even so, the group played rock gigs well into 1970 as Spice before making it all official.

Signature songs: *Wizard, Easy Living, Lady In Black*
Insight songs: *Rain, Gypsy*

THE USED

In early January 2001, three Utah musicians had songs but no singer. They held auditions that were less than productive and asked an acquaintance, Bert McCracken, if he wanted to take a recording home to work on some lyrics. His stellar efforts were met with an instant offer to front the band, and they recorded a demo. A year later, the group was signed to Reprise Records based on the strength of the song, "Box Full of Sharp Objects".

They chose the name, The Used, because most of them were homeless during 2001. They'd slept on couches, raided fridges, and bummed rides from friends, who reported feeling used.

Signature songs: *All That I've Got, I Caught Fire*
Insight song: *I'm A Fake*

V

VAMPIRE WEEKEND
Singer Ezra Koenig was trying to make a *Lost Boys*-esque vampire movie called *Vampire Weekend* set in Cape Cod. The movie never got off the ground but his music did, and he held on to the title of the long-lost film.
Signature songs: *Step, Oxford Comma*
Insight song: *A Punk*

VANILLA FUDGE
Long Island, New York, was treated to the birth of the Electric Pigeons in 1965. A revved-up cover band with more soul than heaven's blues bar, the group gigged relentlessly up and down the East Coast, which included lugging around the organ of front man, Mark Stein. In 1966, they recorded eight demos called *While The Whole World Was Eating Vanilla Fudge* as Mark Stein and The Pigeons.

Meanwhile, they rented themselves out as backup singers for lady groups they'd already covered. In fact, it was their live performance of "You Keep Me Hangin' On" by The Supremes that landed them a producer. Next, their demo landed them a contract with Atco. There was only one problem, the label requested a name change. I bet you're

ahead of the reveal here by now, but the band went with their collective favorite ice cream flavor, and the title of their heretofore biggest recording effort.
Signature song: *You Keep Me Hanging On*
Insight song: *Your Time Is Gonna Come*

THE VELVET UNDERGROUND

The Velvet Underground is a Michael Leigh novel about the secret sexual subculture of the 1960s. It was also the ideal name for a band managed by Andy Warhol. He also made The Velvet Underground house band for his collective art club, The Factory. The group was weird and fearless, which was perfect for New York City in the mid-sixties. Or any time in New York, for that matter.
Signature songs: *Sweet Jane, Heroine, After Hours*
Insight song: *Femme Fatale*

VERTICAL HORIZON

I always thought this band name was a euphemism for vagina, but the official story on their website's FAQs says otherwise. Founding member Keith Kane was writing down names on one of those Magic Slate kid's pads, where you can lift the cellophane and erase what you wrote or drew from the bottom up. He was in someone's backyard and wrote out the words, *vertical pool*. He then lifted the page to replace the word pool with other ideas, and settled on *horizon*. The group plays alternative rock, but have a very polished and powerful sound.

Signature song: *Everything You Want*
Insight songs: *Song For Someone, Send It Up, I'm Still Here*

VERUCA SALT

Grunge rockers from Chicago, best known for their single "Seether" which, as we all know by now, was chosen as a band name by one of their contemporaries.

Their own name was lifted from the Roald Dahl children's classic novel, *Charlie and the Chocolate Factory*. Veruca Salt is the brat deemed a "bad egg" in both the film and the book.

Signature songs: *Seether, Volcano Girls*
Insight songs: *All Hail Me, Laughing In The Sugar Bowl, The Museum Of Broken Relationships*

VIOLENT FEMMES

This band name, like the Smashing Pumpkins, came way before the music. Brian Ritchie came up with it even before Gordon Gano joined to form Milwaukee, Wisconsin's prodigal band. Come to think of it, I'm surprised I don't hear more of their music being played at Green Bay Packers games. No, "Add It Up", of course, but surely "Gone Daddy Gone" would serve nicely as a stadium taunt.

Calling someone a femme in Milwaukee in the seventies was like calling someone a queer. No doubt the slight-built boys heard the slur frequently. The end result was an angry but vulnerable folk/punk poetry that granted their debut album near instant cult status. Their first five albums are near perfection and, like with The Clash, that's where the magic ended. Although *Freak Magnet* was okay.

Signature songs: *Kiss Off, Add It Up, Blister In The Sun, American Music*
Insight songs: *Country Death Song, Fat, Girl Trouble*

VOICE FARM

Charly Brown grew up in Portland, Oregon. After a brief stint in New York City, he moved back to the Pacific Northwest. While corresponding with friends Gary Miles and Barbie White, who lived in San Francisco, he signed one postcard "Help – I'm trapped in a Portuguese voice farm!"

When he eventually joined his friends in the bay area, they'd remembered his comment and decided it would be a great band name, minus the Portuguese. Their funny/funky/trippy music is dripping with sexuality and, according to Charly, is influenced by the Canadian band, General Idea.

Signature songs: *Free Love, Hey Free Thinker*
Insight songs: *King Of The Rat Race, My Idea*

W

THE WALLFLOWERS

This group entered a photo shoot as The Apples but, at one point, the photographer had them all lined up like wallflowers and referred to them as such. The band renamed themselves and played L.A. clubs, including an extended engagement at the famed Kibitz Room at Canter's Delicatessen.

This is Jakob Dylan's band. He is the son of songwriting legend Bob Dylan but refused to over-promote that fact and deliberately kept a low profile. He was so low profile that The Wallflowers eponymous debut album flopped, and they had a mutual split with Virgin Records.

Dylan reformed the band and had two huge hits "6th Avenue Heartache" in 1996, and "One Headlight" in 1997. I saw them in concert when they toured with Counting Crows. Both bands impressed.

Signature songs: *One headlight, Three Marlenas*
Insight song: *Reboot The Mission (with Mick Jones).*

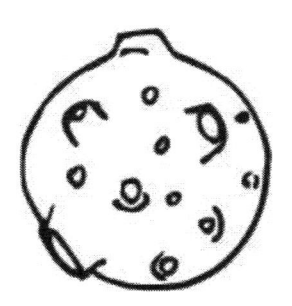

WALK THE MOON

This Cincinnati, Ohio, band formed in 2006, and took their name from the Police song "Walking on the Moon." They cast a wide net musically, and can range from super dancy to super

angsty. Either way, critics and fans have yet to be disappointed.
Signature songs: *Quesadilla, Shut Up and Dance*
Insight songs: *Jenny, I Can Lift A Car, Tiger Teeth*

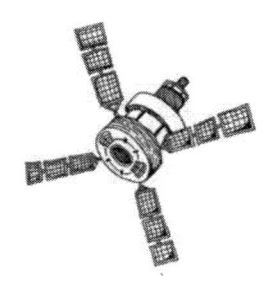

WANG CHUNG
Properly spelled, huang chung, this is the Chinese term for yellow bell, and represents the first note in the Chinese classical scale. London new wave rockers Nick Feldman and Nick Hues liked the way it sounded, literally.
Signature song: *Everybody Have Fun Tonight*
Insight song: *Space Junk*

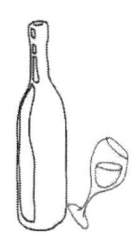

WAR
These kings of Los Angeles had cars pumping their music long before the 1975 hit "Low Rider" turned us all into badasses behind the wheel.
Originally called The Creators in 1968, and described as "Afro-Cuban-funk-groove" most of the members were drafted into the Vietnam War. The remaining members became the band Nightshift and sang backup for then L.A. Rams player, Deacon Jones.
Producer Jerry Goldstein noticed their potential and realized that they were dealing with the personal impacts of war on the band. He suggested re-branding in a way that owned the emotion, and connected them with ex-

Animals singer, Eric Burdon. It was Eric who introduced them to harmonica player Lee Oskar, whose playing would become one of the most recognizable aspects of War's sound and style.

Signature songs: *Spill The Wine, Low Rider, Why Can't We Be Friends*

Insight song: *Galaxy*

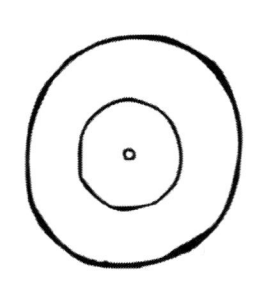

WAX (WAX U.K. in America)

After working with 10cc on their album *Ten out of 10*, songwriter and keyboardist Andrew Gold was asked to officially join the band. He declined, and the band broke up soon after.

Andrew was then invited by Graham Gouldman to visit and ended up staying with him for seven months. They wrote an album's worth of songs and formed a band called World In Action. They released a single, changed their name to Common Knowledge, and released that same single again.

When they signed with RCA Records, they chose the name WAX, as in the slang name for a vinyl record. Getting your music pressed to wax is a big deal.

They added the U.K. for American releases to avoid conflicts with another existing band in the states.

Signature songs: *Bridge To Your Heart, Alright Tonight*

Insight songs: *American English, Share the Glory, Bug In My Machine*

WEEZER

Lead singer Rivers Cuomo has asthma, and, as a kid, his friends called him, you guessed it, Weezer. His band name is him owning it. (Hey, just like the band War did. It's amazing about the alphabetical coincidences. Like, did you notice that the big songs from John Hughes movies came from bands that start with the letter *s*? Weird.)

Weezer is often dismissed as dork rock, but they're the real deal. As punk as Bad Religion, as nuanced as R.E.M., as amusing as Fountains Of Wayne. Seriously, these guys are underrated.

Signature songs: *Buddy Holly, Hash Pipe, Beavery Hills, Island in the Sun*

Insight songs: *Get Right, Love Is the Answer, Go Away, Troublemaker, A Little Bit Of Love*

WHAM!

As schoolmates in Bushy, England, Andrew Ridgeley and George Michael formed a short-lived ska band called The Executive. Overflowing with talent and charisma, they caught the attention of Innervision Records. Wanting to make a big first impression on the music industry, the duo picked the name Wham!

Signature songs: *Wake Me Up Before You Go-Go, Careless Whisper*

Insight song: *Everything She Wants*

THE WHITE STRIPES

Named after the white stripes on a peppermint candy by this once married duo of Meg and Jack White. (He took her name, and it was she who named the band after her favorite treat.) Their debut album has that candy as CD art.

They're from Detroit and play garage rock, with a bit of blues thrown in for good measure. Some of the most innovative songwriting of the new millennium.

Signature songs: *Seven Nation Army, Hardest Button To Button, Icky Thump*

Insight songs: *Fell In Love With A Girl, Catch Hell Blues, Rag And Bone*

WHITE ZOMBIE

This band formed in New York City in 1985 and, just when they got success with their third and fourth albums - *La Sexorcisto: Devil Music Volume One* and *Astro Creep 2000*, they broke up because Rob Zombie and bandmate, Sean Yseult, broke off their romantic relationship. Not everyone can pull off the Fleetwood Mac thing, including Fleetwood Mac.

Their band name was taken from the 1932 Bela Lugosi movie *White Zombie.*

Signature song: *More Human Than Human*

Insight song: *Welcome To Planet Motherfucker*

THE WHO

This is the story of a band who had the name, changed the name, then reclaimed the name. For years, they played as The Detours but, despite being popular in London, they couldn't get any global attention. It was decided that they should change their name to something more interesting. Guitarist Pete Townshend suggested The Who, relaying that any time he told his grandmother about a new band, she always responded with "The who?"

They were signed, but their band manager renamed them The High Numbers in support of their only single "I'm the Face." (Face was slang for put together well.) The single flopped and EMI dropped the band, who subsequently sacked their manager, focused on "Maximum R&B," and re-renamed themselves The Who again.

It was about this time that Pete Townshend smashed his first guitar at a gig in the Railway Hotel. It was quite by accident. He lifted his guitar up over his head after their encore and it smashed against the low ceiling. Pete was incensed by the damage to his guitar and smashed the ruined instrument against the stage. The crowd went wild. A week later their show sold more tickets than ever before, and everyone expected to see another smashing encore. The band had a name. They had a sound. And now, they had a gimmick. Of course, they hit it big.

Signature songs: *My Generation, Baba O'Riley*
Insight songs: *Bargain, You Better You Bet*

WIDESPREAD PANIC

Lead guitarist and band founder Mike Houser earned the nickname Panic as a teenager. Legend has it that he not only embraced the moniker but announced one day that he no longer wanted to be just Panic, but Widespread Panic. This is yet another boundary breaking band from Athens.

Signature song: *Porch Song*
Insight song: *Coconut*

WILCO

As in "Roger Wilco," radio shorthand for "Roger that, will comply." Lead singer and guitarist Jeff Tweedy thought it was an ironic name for a rock and roll band, especially a Chicago rock and roll band as Chicago musicians are especially known for pushing limits and ignoring traditional tropes. Chicago goes its own way. That's why there's a different section for blues and Chicago blues.

Wilco has soul, but they definitely don't play the blues. They're an alternative rock band with fits of emo and punk in them.

Signature song: *A Shot In The Arm*
Insight song: *Jesus Ect.*

WU-TANG CLAN

Holy crap! Something good finally came out of Staten Island! No offense Pete Davidson, I'm a fan. (And no, this isn't like an Ariana Grande song where you get money just because I mentioned your name. Or is it? I don't really know for sure.) Just in case, nobody show this book to Pete Davidson.

Wu-Tang Clan is one of the most revered hip-hop acts of all time. And that's saying a lot because the East Coast has a long list of legends. Half of which ended up in this band. Here's the rundown of original members: Ol' Dirty Bastard, RZA, Method Man, GZA, Ghostface Killa, Masta Killa, Inspectah Deck, and U-God.

The name was inspired by the 1981 Kung-fu movie *Shaolin and Wu Tang*. But the Tang Clan isn't fictional. They are one of the Five Great Clans of the New Territories. Which is to say, one of five great families that settled in the new territories of Hong Kong. (This is like 12th Century shit. And no, I'm not trying to add filler to my book just because my potential publisher asked me to get to 40,000 words. Although that business with Pete Davidson might definitely make you think so. Great. Now I probably owe him even more money.)

Signature songs: *Triumph, C.R.E.A.M., Method Man, Protect Ya Neck*

Insight song: *The Mystery Of Chessboxin'*

X

X-RAY SPEX

London punk rock is not done with us yet. Singer/songwriter Poly Styrene shuffled musicians around while she regularly played at the famed Man In The Moon pub. They chose their name for the American novelty toy, X-Ray Specs, advertised in fifties magazines. Notorious underachievers, they only released one album, 1978's *Germ Free Adolescence*, before breaking up for seventeen years.

Signature song: *Oh Bondage Up Yours*
Insight song: *I Am A Poseur*

XTC

A fascinating thing happened with this Swindon band's biggest hit, "Dear God." The song first appeared as a non-album B side to the single "Grass," but received way more airplay and became their breakout song. There are a few instances like this in rock and roll, where the B side becomes a bigger hit than the single it was intended to support. Most notably include "Tequila" "Rock Around the Clock" and "Unchained Melody."

Now, about the band name. Founding member Andy Partridge saw a Jimmy Durante movie where the actor exclaimed "That's it! I'm in ecstasy!" Andy heard it as

"I'm in XTC!" Before the band settled on that name, they also considered Dukes of Stratosphere, Terry and the Lovemen, and The Three Wisemen.
Signature songs: *Dear God, Mayor Of Simpleton*
Insight song: *Life Begins At The Hop*

THE XX

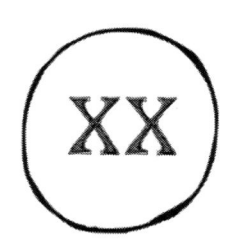

This band got their start in a Wandsworth, London high school. Their name comes from a Norse rune, Inguz. Symbolized by xx, the rune represents male energy and fertility. Its translation is the common phrase we know as "Where there's a will, there's a way." The group's stripped down indie sound boasts two vocalists, creative songwriting, and stamina. Lots of stamina.
Signature songs: *Crystalised, Angels, I Dare You*
Insight song: *On Hold (*Jamie xx Remix*)*

Y

THE YARDBIRDS

In Jack Kerouac's 1957 novel *On The Road*, train yard hobos were referred to as Yardbirds. Legendary jazz saxophone player Charlie Parker was also nicknamed Yardbird. In 1963, Jimmy Page was leading a band called The Metropolitan Blues Quartet and changed their name to The Yardbirds to better capture interest in the London blues scene.

Signature songs: *For Your Love, Train Kept A Rollin'*
Insight song: *I'm A Man*

YAZOO (YAZ in America)

The second band started by Vince Clarke. When he quit Depeche Mode, he was worried that he wouldn't have a deal with Mute Records anymore, so he answered an advertisement in a local musician's magazine. He connected with blues vocalist, Alison Moyet, whom he had been acquainted with since childhood, and asked her to sing on his demo of a song called "Only You." The label liked it, and the new duo was encouraged to collaborate on a full album.

The name Yazoo was taken from a blues record label, which led to a lawsuit against them.

They went with Yaz, mostly because of their American

success, but Vince never liked the name. Allison never liked all the synthesizers, and they split up after only eighteen months and two albums. Vince went on to create the band Erasure with Andy Bell.

Signature songs: *Only You, Don't Go, Bad Connection*
Insight songs: *In My Room, State Farm (Madhouse Mix)*

YEAH YEAH YEAHS

New York vernacular has produced many gems, but "yeah, yeah, yeah," was something this band heard a lot growing up. They chose the expression as a name in homage to NYC, no matter where the music took them.

They have a real garage/punk/dance thing going on. Like New York, you get a lot of bang for your buck with these guys and gals.

Signature song: *Maps*
Insight song: *Heads Will Roll*

YELLO

This is a Swiss duo, best known for their song "Oh Yeah" which is featured in the 1986 John Hughes film *Ferris Bueller's Day Off*. Their name is not meant to conjure images of the color yellow. Instead, it's an example of a neologism, and means "a yelled, hello." This phrase was uttered by vocalist Dieter Meier and it was decided it should represent the band.

Signature song: *Oh Yeah*
Insight song: *Limbo*

YELLOWCARD
Even casual fans of soccer probably know that being shown a yellow card means a foul has been committed. Growing up in Jacksonville, the band and their friends used the term to call out party fouls.

The group have since moved to Los Angeles, which has a greater appreciation for the punk rock scene. Yellowcard is more emo than punk at times, but they can also get downright metal.

Signature songs: *Ocean Avenue, Only One, Way Away*
Insight song: *Rough Landing Holly*

YES
In 1968, a London band called Ants Farming Indonesia were considering a name change to something a little more relatable. While funny, funky band names were all the rage in the early sixties, these musicians felt that bands with names like The Who and The Doors appeared more powerful.

They brainstormed simple names, but also wanted something with a lot of weight to it. Jon Davison suggested Life. Chris Squire tried World. Peter Banks kept saying "Yes, yes, yes." Encouraged, the other two kept coming up with ideas before they realized that Peter was actually suggesting Yes as a band name. His choice won the night.

The group became giants of progressive rock, with some albums consisting of only three or four epic songs. Like Pink Floyd, their live shows became the stuff of legend.
Signature songs: *Owner Of A Lonely Heart, Roundabout, Close To The Edge*
Insight songs: *Changes, Magnification, Leave It*

YO LA TENGO
This Hoboken, New Jersey, band chose the Spanish phrase for "I have it" because of an old baseball story about the New York Mets. In the 1962 baseball season, center fielder Richie Ashburn and shortstop Elio Chacón kept crashing into each other. Elio didn't speak English, and didn't understand when Richie kept yelling "I got it! I got it!"

At a team meeting, it was decided that Richie would yell, "*Yo la tengo!*" going forward. Unfortunately, Frank Thomas, the team's left-fielder, missed that crucial meeting and ran right over poor Richie in the very next game. After getting up, Frank was heard asking "What the hell is a yellow tango?"

Great band, with a great story, and I will also mention that they have great album names as well, my favorite being, *I'm Not Afraid of You, And I Will Beat Your Ass.*
Signature song: *Sugarcube*
Insight song: *Watch Out For Me Ronnie*

Z

ZEDD

This Russian born, German raised DJ and producer had an album come out in 2015 called *Colors*, which is one of the most perfect albums I own. His birth name is Anton Zaslavski and his stage name is a modification of his childhood nickname, Zed (which is how Europeans pronounced the first letter of his last name since the name itself was a tongue twister). At school, he was always last in line.

Signature song: *Beautiful Now*
Insight song: *True Colors*

THE ZOMBIES

Members of the band met as students in St. Albans, northwest of London. They originally called themselves The Mustangs but discovered two bands already fighting over that name. Rod Argent, the band's keyboardist, has said that it was former member Paul Arnold who came up with the name, The Zombies. In 1962, the word was not widely known and carried a lot of Haitian mystery with it. It was a risky move.

Signature songs: *Time Of The Season, She's Not There*
Insight song: *Care Of Cell 44*

ZEBRAHEAD

Drummer Ed Udhus and guitarist Greg Bergdorf formed a band called 409 in La Habra, California. They shared rehearsal space with bassist Ben Osmundson, who was playing in a band called 3-Ply. Another band, Once There, fronted by Justin Mauriello also practiced in the same building. The three of them began experimenting together and pursued a pop-punk-rap-rock sound. They chose their name in haste to secure a gig. But it stood out, as did their music.

They took their name from the 1992 Anthony Drazan film, *Zebrahead*. The word is meant to be a derogatory term for half Black, half white.

Signature song: *If You're Looking For Your Knife I Think My Back Found It*
Insight song: *All My Friends Are Nobodies*

ZZ TOP

Originally a blues band, this Texas trio wanted to name themselves ZZ King as a tribute to their favorite blues artist, B.B. King. They later changed the name to ZZ Top to avoid confusion, but the "Top" was still B.B. King related since they were tipping their hats to the top idol of the band.

Signature songs: *Sharp Dressed Man, Legs, Gimme All Your Lovin'*
Insight song: *I Thank You*

ALSO FROM LOCKLEAR BOOKS

Morgan Locklear & Jennifer Locklear

Exposure

Morgan Locklear

Connection
The Apple Wagon
Start Me Up: How That Band Got That Name They Got

Jennifer Locklear

Constellation
Chaos

ABOUT THE AUTHOR

Morgan Locklear is a novelist and musician living on the Oregon coast with his wife, author Jennifer Locklear. The two write books both together and separately with multiple charity anthologies, and guest appearances in short story collections.

Morgan has performed in, or directed over thirty community theatre shows in Newport, and has recorded a half dozen albums with the bands, Cool Beans, Miracle Max, and Absolute Value. You can search his name on Spotify and find all sorts of wild stuff.

He writes romance adventures with a focus on humor, and few ghosts thrown in from time to time. He has a thing for ghosts, trains, and New York City, culminated in his debut novel, Connection.

Morgan is a legally blind triplet, which means that growing up, he could see just well enough to get himself into trouble, but had plenty of sisters to bail him out. (Not literally, of course.)

Morgan loves Seinfeld, Mel Brooks, punk rock, and big historical novels. His future is bright with three more books on deck, two sequels planned for this project, and more short stories in the works than all the gumballs in Graceland.

SPECIAL THANKS

There are several people who were instrumental (pun intended) in the success of this project. Pat Todd, who is a musical hero of mine, wrote the introduction. Chris Reid supplied valuable content. Marla Esposito edited the thing twice. And, Lindsey Gray crafted the perfect design both inside and out. Lindsey, you are a wonderful artist.

Big-time thanks to: Stephanie DeLamater Phillips, Shari Ivey, Jim "Doc" Watson, Dany Oakes, Johnny Siera, Karen Komarinski, Joyce Pennington, Don Applebaum, Phil Nicholas, Sue and Andy Swords, Jason and Jessala White, Stephan, and everyone in The Vinyl Frontier. (Also Pete Davidson, just in case.)

Thank you to Larry and Suzanne Locklear for constantly telling me what a good idea this book was.

Finally, I would like to thank my wife, Jennifer Locklear. She always puts in tons of time working on my books instead of her own. I love you, and I'm lucky to have you.

-MOG

Made in the USA
Columbia, SC
07 July 2024

b852d72e-37b7-496a-b41f-4c0ee5e10ff6R04